Wonder is a story we're able to tell ourselves, and that story is one we can use to change our lives (and the world) for the better. This is a powerful, generous, and unforgettable book about our ability to care and to lead.

SETH GODIN, author of *The Practice*

The Wonder Switch pulls you in and ignites your imagination. It's a book that will inspire other books, a gift that will inspire more gifts, a wonder that will inspire even more wonders. While I'm grateful for what Harris III has created with this book, I'm even more excited to see all the magic it uncovers in the many readers it is sure to find.

BRAD MONTAGUE, *New York Times* bestselling
author, creator of *Kid President*

Harris's energy for life is contagious, his creativity is a force, and this book will leave you inevitably inspired. *The Wonder Switch* gave me permission—and backed it up with scientific research—to keep dreaming at forty-four as if I were four. We so often lose our wonder as we age, yet bringing it back into our lives gives a positive boost to ourselves, our relationships, our work, and our homes. I dare you to pick up this book. And then I dare you to try to put it down.

CANDACE CAMERON BURE, actress, producer,
New York Times bestselling author

Illusionists aren't supposed to share their tricks, but I've spent ten years watching Harris create wonder in rooms around the world, and he's finally revealing what it takes. He's one of the smartest, most creative people I've ever met, and fortunately for both of us, he's also one of the most generous. You won't get better at cards or making things disappear, but what you get in this book is far more powerful—a guide back to wonder. If you feel like your life could use a bit more love, joy, belonging, and purpose, I dare you to crack open *The Wonder Switch*.

JON ACUFF, *New York Times* bestselling author of *Finish*

Harris has offered us a sacred glimpse behind the curtain of real magic. His life's calling pours out of these pages and opens us to wide-eyed wonder as an agency of transformation! Encounter this book and be changed!

DANIELLE STRICKLAND, author, speaker, advocate, leader

Wonder seems illusive, like something we may have known as a child but was beaten out of us by the real world. But in *The Wonder Switch*, Harris III is a rare storyteller who can help us rediscover the living stream of wonder that flows within our grasp. It's a work of eye-opening insight, wrapped in a moving memoir that makes this essential reading for the wonder-seeker in us all.

DON HAHN, legendary Disney producer

In *The Wonder Switch*, Harris III weaves the themes of wonder, story, narrative, and personal transformation into a magical tale. He guides you into the essential nature of our shared human experience and then hands you the keys. Keys that empower you to choose your experience and to write and rewrite your own story, over and over and over, creating a life, and a world, from wonder. If you are looking for a new set of keys for your life, this book is for you.

GILLIAN FERRABEE, founder and president
of Kite Parade Innovation Agency

THE
WONDER
SWITCH

THE WONDER

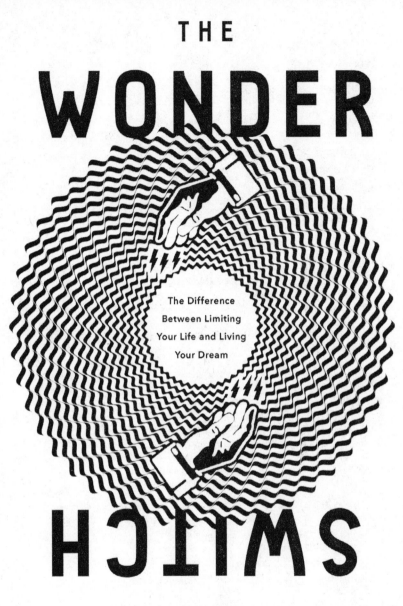

The Difference
Between Limiting
Your Life and Living
Your Dream

SWITCH

HARRIS III

ZONDERVAN
THRIVE

ZONDERVAN THRIVE

The Wonder Switch
Copyright © 2020 by Robert C. Harris, III

Requests for information should be addressed to:
Zondervan, *3900 Sparks Dr. SE, Grand Rapids, Michigan 49546*

Zondervan titles may be purchased in bulk for educational, business, fundraising, or sales promotional use. For information, please email SpecialMarkets@Zondervan.com.

ISBN 978-0-310-36102-2 (audio)

Library of Congress Cataloging-in-Publication Data

Names: Harris, III, 1983-author.
Title: The wonder switch / Harris III.
Description: Grand Rapids : Zondervan Thrive, [2020] | Includes bibliographical references. | Summary: "In The Wonder Switch, professional illusionist Harris III draws from brain science and his expertise as a magician turned storyteller to take us on a journey back to magic—not the stuff of sleight of hand that he performs on stage, but real magic: love, hope, joy, belonging, meaning, and purpose—which transforms every facet of our work and lives"—Provided by publisher.
Identifiers: LCCN 2020023695 (print) | LCCN 2020023696 (ebook) | ISBN 9780310360995 (hardcover) | ISBN 9780310361008 (ebook)
Subjects: LCSH: Wonder. | Emotions. | Well-being.
Classification: LCC BF575.A9 H37 2020 (print) | LCC BF575.A9 (ebook) | DDC 158.1—dc23
LC record available at https://lccn.loc.gov/2020023695
LC ebook record available at https://lccn.loc.gov/2020023696

Zondervan Thrive, an imprint of Zondervan, publishes books that empower readers with insightful, expert-driven ideas for a life of thriving in today's world.

Cover design: Spencer Fuller / Faceout Studio
Cover illustrations: CSA Images / Getty Images; mrnvb / Shuttterstock
Interior design: Denise Froehlich

Printed in the United States of America

---

20 21 22 23 24   /LSC/   10 9 8 7 6 5 4 3 2 1

To Jude, Everly, and Mylo
Thank you for reawakening my wonder
and teaching me what real magic is

Contents

Foreword

Until one is committed, there is hesitancy, the chance to draw back. Concerning all acts of initiative (and creation), there is one elementary truth, the ignorance of which kills countless ideas and splendid plans: that the moment one definitely commits oneself, then Providence moves too. All sorts of things occur to help one that would never otherwise have occurred. A whole stream of events issues from the decision, raising in one's favor all manner of unforeseen incidents and meetings and material assistance, which no man could have dreamed would have come his way. Whatever you can do, or dream you can do, begin it. Boldness has genius, power, and magic in it. Begin it now.

W. H. MURRAY

My life's journey is a clear example and proof of concept that the Transformation Map found in this book is not simply a whimsical idea or hypothesis haphazardly shared for the reader to casually consume. I am proof that the ideas Harris lays out for you are feasible and verifiable.

To use words that you will soon read, my "old story" was ruled by worry. My parents chose their addiction over raising three sons.

The pinnacle moment of their neglect resulted in the three of us being "rescued" by a stranger, shuttled down to a Greyhound bus station in Bowling Green, Virginia, and placed on a bus alone. My older brother was eight years old, I was six years old, and my younger brother was three years old. We were sent on a two-hundred-plus-mile, one-way trip to my grandparents' house in Philadelphia.

Soon came another inciting incident and, along with it, a spark that led to awe and back to the truth, eventually restoring my narrative and permitting me to step into a new story.

Without parents in my life, I resorted to learning life lessons from many other sources: businessmen and laborers, winos and alcoholics, drug dealers and users, sport coaches, my peers and old heads at the playground, merchants, war vets, schoolteachers, librarians, custodians, food service workers, and other kids' moms and dads. I learned to be constantly on the lookout for any nugget of insight or wisdom that would assist me on my quest to rise above my suffering and circumstances. Turning ideas into reality became my focus. "I'll show you!" became my daily mantra.

I spent endless hours at the neighborhood playground, school, and the public library. These locales became my sanctuaries. Finding a way to rise above my circumstances and not let my circumstances dictate my destiny was my constant motivation.

Preston Playground was the community epicenter. At that playground, an unimpressive pugilistic moment—a "peace offering" of PB&J—proved to be the catalytic moment in my journey from a dysfunctional and a hardscrabble life to success and a life-long pursuit of significance. Wonder switch . . . ON!

I know firsthand about the transformative power of wonder being switched ON and what it can catalyze—a productive imagination and a Wonder Mindset that is freed by hope and driven by curiosity. Enjoy the read. God speed. Game on! #grit #grace #OMBFF

KEVIN CARROLL
Creativity Expert

Note from the Author

Can I begin with a confession? Writing a book is scary. There's something about putting your thoughts and ideas into print for . . . forever.

The pages that follow are filled with personal stories, and I've written the words that tell them with as much courage and vulnerability as I could muster. Other parts of what you're about to read are based not on my own personal discoveries but on the latest findings in neuroscience and psychology. But here's the thing about science: we learn more and more every day.

To supplement the (hopefully) timeless truths in this book, my team and I have created a workbook designed to accompany your reading. It's filled with questions, prompts, exercises, and more to help you reawaken your wonder and experience all that it has to offer you in your life and your work. Keeping this workbook in a digital format enables us to make updates based on new scientific studies, ensuring that it stays fresh.

We've also created a free assessment to help you identify the current stage of your journey of transformation in an effort to help you focus and maximize your efforts.

Head over to thewonderswitch.com for these resources and more.

Thanks for allowing me to
be part of your journey,

Harris III

CHAPTER 1

Wonder Switch On

The Beginning of Everything You Want

I started performing magic as a kid, back in the 1990s. Though the information age had already arrived, we didn't have that information readily available in our pockets quite yet. For the most part, people were still comfortable living in mystery because Siri and Google weren't around to instantaneously provide answers to all of life's questions. That made it highly enjoyable to create mysteries onstage. It was so much fun that I've spent most of my life traveling around the world performing magic shows in almost forty countries for over two million people, not including appearances on TV or YouTube.

Though my career over the last few years has evolved beyond being an illusionist, I'm still performing magic, but audiences are more averse to wonder in response to that magic than they used to be.

Night after night, before the house lights go down and the show begins, audience members are relaxed. But the moment the emcee prepares the audience for what is to come, there's a shift in the room. People sit up, lean in, and often cross their arms—not just because the show is starting but as if they're preparing to intellectually defend themselves against any chance of being fooled, as if that's what watching a magic show is all about. As I walk onstage, people stare me down, thinking, "All right, Mr. Magic Guy, let's see if you can fool me." Instead of sitting back, relaxing, and enjoying the show—instead of realizing that wonder is one of life's most beautiful experiences—they become wonder-crushers.

We don't do this with any other art form. We don't stare at a painting and shrug off the painter's talent simply because we may "know how she did that." When you watch your favorite musical artist make magic on an instrument, if you're a musician, you never simply crush your awe and wonder by saying, "Even though I can't play guitar like that, I know how he did it. I know those chords."

Knowing how something was accomplished doesn't mean it isn't beautiful or enjoyable to experience. And beautiful things contain elements of mystery, since there is always more to discover. We may want to know all the secrets, and many magicians may even present their illusions as puzzles to be solved, as if they're taunting you with a challenge: "I bet you don't know how I did that." But mysteries are beautiful. Mystery can leave us in wonder. And wonder tells a different story.

The Wonder Switch

Imagine sitting in total darkness but having no idea where you are. You don't know what's around you. You don't know what's behind you. You don't even know what's right in front of your face.

Allow your imagination to explore the scenario. Sitting alone in the darkness may sound nice to you. Or you might wonder what's in the room with you. Is it your worst fear? Or maybe your worst fear *is* that there's absolutely nothing and no one at all. You are completely, utterly alone.

Now imagine a light switch on the wall.

Does the knowledge of that switch give you hope? The lights aren't on yet, which means the world around you has yet to be illuminated. But what if you could find that switch and turn on the lights? You no longer have to be in the dark, because turning on that switch gives you the ability to see.

Wonder is like that light switch. Having the wonder switch on leads to a healthy form of curiosity that is connected to dreaming, innovation, and creativity. The wonder switch also controls how you use your imagination. It doesn't affect whether you use it, because your imagination was at work while you sat in the dark. Wonder simply changes what you use your imagination for. Everything you want, and then some, is on the other side of turning the wonder switch back on.

But what if your wonder switch stays off? What's the cost?

The stakes are high; without wonder, your life is ruled by cynicism, stress, worry, and anxiety. Research shows that your life span will likely be shorter too.[1] Maybe you feel unmoved by this information because you feel apathetic or complacent. But I believe there is still hope, regardless of your current state. That you've cracked open this book and read this far means a voice inside you is saying, "There's more for you," even if that voice has become a faint whisper.

The reality for most of us is that life, and the art of living it, is an ongoing journey of the wonder switch being turned on and off.

We're born with it on. Then a bully on the playground or in your home turns it off. A teacher or coach who affirms the magic inside you turns it back on. Then someone whose own wonder has been crushed, crushes ours. Wonder switch off. On. Off. On. Off.

Years go by, and the gaps between the switch being on or off grow bigger. Then the gaps become like expansive canyons until the wonder of our youth feels like a distant, vague memory. Finally, the switch is worn and rusty, the way most things get when they haven't been used in years. And so we learn to live without it.

We settle. And we allow the wonder that was crushed in us to crush the wonder of those around us.

As you'll find out in the chapters ahead, wonder affects all areas of your life, just like there's no part of darkness that light doesn't illuminate.

If you're struggling at work, wonder can transform your leadership by changing the stories you tell yourself and the stories you lead others to internalize. Wonder permits you to believe in those you lead in new ways, helping you see the magic in others that they have yet to see in themselves.

If you're struggling as a parent, engaging wonder can transform your parenting. It permits you to see the world the way your kids do, gifting you with a healthy dose of empathy and understanding as you try to relate to the stories they're living and telling themselves. Great parents, like great leaders, are wide awake to the world of possibilities, with wonder increasing your ability to help your children step into their authentic selves and live their fullest lives. Without wonder, you run the risk of crushing your kids' wonder and crushing their hopes and dreams in the process.

It doesn't matter if you don't think you're a leader, or if you don't have children, or if you're not married. Everyone, deep down, has the desire to live what they consider to be their version of a creative life. As we'll soon discover, you are already creating, for better or for worse. But wonder can ignite or breathe new life into your creative process, regardless of your creative pursuits. Wonder gives birth to curious exploration that neuroscience connects to innovative thinking. It doesn't take much effort to see all the ways your creativity is connected to other areas of your life. Sure, you can creatively reimagine every facet of your life and work, but you don't have to in order for wonder to work its magic—it impacts even things as seemingly mundane as your personal or family's financial picture, including your ability to crush debt and increase your capacity to give generously to others.

If you're content with the level of success you're currently experiencing in your life and work, that's amazing. There is no single definition for "success"—it feels like a word that should always be in air quotes. To be clear, this isn't a self-help motivational book about becoming an entrepreneur, growing a business, or making more money, though wonder is an essential part of those processes. If growing your business is your dream, this book will serve you well. My hope is that this book, and the wonder it will guide you toward reawakening, will make you a healthier, happier, and better human being. In turn, you'll become a better partner, neighbor, and friend. It will enable you to be released from the nightmares that often haunt you, and permit you to receive love, give love, and be part of collectively changing the future of our world.

Maybe all that sounds a little grandiose. Maybe you're here, reading or listening to these words, because you're struggling to hold on to hope. If so, I have good news—wonder can keep your hope alive. New studies in neurobiology connect wonder to your body's physiology and even your ability to emotionally connect with and empathize with other human beings.[2] Increasing your capacity to give and receive love isn't hyperbole.

Without wonder, our curiosity dies. Instead of adventurously exploring potential solutions to the problems we bump into throughout our lives, we succumb to the pressures that come from being a responsible adult, and we settle for a life filled with stress and anxiety. The feelings of failure produce shame, so we isolate ourselves. And the lack of connection leads to a lack of hope, which breeds complacency. We feel like we aren't enough. We feel like we don't fit in or belong. We feel like the things we desire are forever out of reach.

So many lies. But wonder can lead you to the truth. Wonder is a powerful catalyst for change. It surprises you and, as my friend Brad Montague says, "rescues you from the ordinary."[3] Wonder is the moment when you witness something beautiful and bigger than yourself and know without a doubt that you were made for more. It whispers, "Isn't this extraordinary?" Wonder is more than just a feeling—it is a childlike state that gives you permission to believe in real magic.

By the time you're done with this book, my hope is not only that your wonder will be awakened but that you also feel equipped to cultivate and sustain wonder in your life. There's more hope for that than you may realize, because wonder doesn't exist only on the mountaintops. It exists in the nooks and crannies, in both the joys and sorrows we experience in our journey along the way.

I understand that you may have picked up this book thinking that flipping the wonder switch back on could be done in three simple steps. Unfortunately, as we'll discover together, that isn't how wonder works. But I will equip you with some steps you can take to find yourself in a state of wonder more often and teach you how to develop a Wonder Mindset.

Let's explore a simple framework I've used to help guide countless others through the process of changing the stories they're living, with wonder at the center. To change a story, transformation is required. Transformation happens when an individual or even a collective team at an organization moves from an old story to a new story. As we'll discuss later in this book, the narratives we have adopted as true, whether they're actually true or not, are what shape the stories we tell ourselves. Those stories drive all our thinking and behavior. I've worked with so many people who struggle to make the changes they want to make because they're stuck in an old story.

Here's what that process looks like, in the form of something I like to call the Transformation Map:

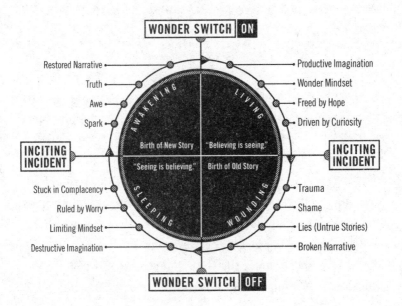

The Wonder Switch is at the center of this transformational storytelling process. And while this book clearly focuses on the role of wonder, we'll also explore the power of story. As the map shows, stories and wonder go hand in hand.

It's important to know that it's entirely possible to be at different places on the map in different parts of your life. I've coached many leaders who live wide awake to wonder at work but are highly cynical and stuck in complacency when it comes to their personal relationships, dating life, or marriage. Others may embrace possibility in their parenting, for example, but assume the worst when it comes to their current role at work.

We are complex storytelling creatures with multiple narratives. Many of us have developed religious narratives, political narratives, financial narratives, relational narratives, health narratives, and other narratives that guide our lives.

When we change the untrue stories we tell ourselves and embrace the radical self-inquiry required to make the leap to a new story, we'll find truth, hope, and live a more whole, authentic life, allowing us to experience the love and belonging we so strongly desire. We can't get there without wonder, because wonder is what gives us permission to believe—to imagine that a magical new story is possible—long before we're able to see that story come to life.

The fact that this map is laid out in a circle makes this process of change a never-ending cycle. Often just when things in our lives are going well and we like the story we find ourselves in, inciting incidents can blindside us against our will, causing trauma, wreaking havoc, and sucking us back down into the bottom of the circle. As we work toward healing and grow in wisdom, we can spend more and more of our lives in the top half of the circle and become better equipped to respond to the incidents that so often become catalysts for negative change.

We'll come back to this map a few times throughout this book. For now, what's an old story you currently feel stuck in? Can you identify that story and where you are in this process of taking steps toward a story driven by wonder?

Maybe you feel shame from something in your past or still experience the lingering effects of unresolved trauma. Maybe the lies you've been tricked into believing led to a broken narrative, and the limiting beliefs, worry, and cynicism keep you from imagining anything remotely hopeful, so you've settled, grown comfortably numb, and are now stuck in complacency. If that's where you find yourself, get ready. Sometimes it takes only a spark to ignite your awe and lead you back to a place of wonder, where more is possible than you currently imagine.

The Beginning of Everything You Want

What story do you want to come to life that currently exists only in your imagination? Seriously, if you could wish for anything, what would you wish for?

Did you ever have that conversation as a kid? We used to ask each other about wishes all the time in school. Maybe it was being born in the eighties and the timing of the release of *Aladdin*. Or maybe all kids think about what they'd wish for and out of curiosity ask their friends, in case there's a better wish they haven't come up with yet. When you're seven, you never know when a genie's going to appear out of nowhere, so you've gotta be prepared, ya know?

Honestly, I can't even remember what my childhood wishes

were, other than the usual "more wishes," which was obviously disallowed every time it came up. But if I ever received a wish now as an adult, I'd wish for wisdom. It's what I'm consistently striving for, begging mentors for, praying for, and feel like I never have enough of. And if you think about it, wishing to gain wisdom is almost the real-world equivalent of wishing for more wishes.

Think about something you want. Anything. What is it? It may not be what immediately comes to mind.

For example, an easy answer to that question might be something like "more money." But is it money you really want, or what you imagine that money will give you? Is it money, or is it financial freedom, or the resources to do more good in the world? Or is it that you're under the impression that if you just had the money, you could live the kind of lifestyle that offers you more friends, solving any loneliness you're currently feeling?

Wisdom peels back the layers and offers more depth, allowing you to sidestep the foolishness and guiding you to what can truly fulfill you. Wisdom helps us come to the realization that often what we think we want is not always what it seems. Wisdom helps us see that there's almost always more to the story.

As wisdom peels back those layers, taking you to greater depths, what will you then find yourself wanting? Possibly closer relationships or a better marriage? A more meaningful company? More contentment? More joy and purpose in your life? If you had wisdom, couldn't you have what you want by being able to identify what's getting in the way and the steps required to attain it? I think so. What if all the magic you're searching for (and you are indeed searching for it, whether you realize it or not) could be had if only you possessed the wisdom to know where to find it and how to grasp it?

So how do we find wisdom? How do we become wise?

Socrates said, "Wisdom begins in wonder."

If he was right, then maybe becoming wise begins with the reawakening of wonder.

Is it possible that one of the reasons our world seems so lacking in wisdom is that we've lost our sense of wonder? I don't think it would take much convincing for anyone to look around and come to the same conclusion. You can witness foolishness in a few quick clicks on YouTube or by watching just a few minutes of television. Flip through the channels—it's everywhere. You could also read the comments sections or Twitter replies of just about any tweet or other social media thread. Especially threads about politics. Or if you're like me, you can simply look in the mirror. I like to think I'm a smart guy, but the truth is, like a child who acts out because negative attention is better than no attention, I act foolish sometimes.

So much in the world around us conspires against our wonder in an attempt to crush it, replacing our curiosity with complacency. Those who fight to crush our wonder prefer we stay in line, not ask questions, and settle for the status quo. If they succeed at that goal, we won't cause a ruckus or be part of the disruption that awakens others from their slumber. As we leave a state of wonder, we pivot to a place of worry.

If wisdom begins in wonder, then worry gives birth to foolishness. Some of the biggest regrets of my life arose from decisions I made when I was cynical or scared. And the older I get, the more I realize that cynicism is just my pretending I'm not afraid. If you spend your life gripped by fear and worry, complacency will only lead to another version of regret—getting to the end of your life with a long list of shattered dreams rooted in things you wish you *would* have done. Either way, this is not the way of the wise.

I used to think the big question was, Do we start out foolish and work to become wise, or do we start out wise and grow up to become foolish? But maybe the truth is that we're born awake to wonder, and as our wonder is crushed, the hope of wisdom—and all that comes with it—slowly fades away.

You have to admit, our culture's growing in foolishness is somewhat ironic because we now know more than humanity has known at any other time in history. We've been in the information age for decades. We seemingly find the answer to any problem with a simple online search. If something is a mystery to us, a video explaining the mysterious is at our fingertips, all in a device that fits into our pocket. We've been psychologically conditioned to no longer value mystery, making wonder uncomfortable. After all, why be amazed by something when you can simply "understand" it? There wouldn't be reason to be amazed if understanding how something works meant losing our capacity to continue to marvel at the thing we now understand.

Clearly, information and wisdom are not equals. Information is finite. Wisdom is infinite. Access to information does not automatically lead to positive transformation. The age of information has led to living in an abundance of certainty. But that abundance of certainty has clouded our vision and permitted us to live under the illusion that we are wise. As a professional illusionist, I see this tension play out every night I'm onstage.

Not All Secrets Are Meant to Be Kept

When my wife turned thirty, a big group of friends got together and threw her a surprise party. We rented a cool, historic old building in downtown Nashville and had everyone dress up in twenties fashion, and I even hired a ragtime piano player and variety performers to complete the part-vaudeville, part-speakeasy vibe we were going for. The moment she walked into the room and everyone yelled, "Surprise!" it was as if we were saying, "Hey, Kate! We love you!"

Can you imagine how hard it was to keep that whole thing a secret? Sometimes the not knowing is beautiful. Not knowing leaves room for surprises. A surprise party says, "Surprise! You are loved." If there are no secrets or mysteries, there is no room for wonder. And if there is no wonder, we're left without wisdom. Lacking wisdom, we never discover the magical life we're each capable of living.

As we learn to embrace the mysteries of life and the world around us, we learn to wrestle with the tension—the tension found in the fact that some mysteries are meant to remain a mystery, and some are meant to be solved. After all, not all secrets should be kept.

Whenever you don't know something or find yourself getting "tricked," you may feel dumb or uncomfortable. But these experiences can also give birth to wonder, and wisdom begins in wonder. But I don't want you merely to begin. I don't want you to turn your wonder switch back on only for a while. My hope is for it to stay on so you can live a life beyond your wildest imagination. I also hope you lead others around you to do the same. But for wonder to stay alive, we must identify the narrative that threatens to crush it.

To grasp the power of the stories we tell ourselves, let's venture back to the mysterious land of make-believe, to a world where the monsters who chased us didn't get to win—where our swords slayed the dragons and our demons couldn't come back to haunt us. How does that sound?

Impossible, you say? You might be right. That's a world I *wish* we could go back to regularly. Sure, we could imagine it. In the world of imagination, literally anything is possible. I don't know about you, but the world where the monsters who chased us didn't get to win—that world didn't survive my childhood. And demons came back regularly to haunt me, long before I became an adult.

In this book, you'll reawaken your wonder, that childlike wonder you often felt when you were a little kid, before this world robbed it and took it far away. But, of course, we can't blame it all on "the world." We are complicit in the untrue stories we tell ourselves. We need to take responsibility and spend less time pointing fingers. Yet even if you are responsible for telling yourself many stories filled with falsehoods, it does not change the fact that you've been robbed of wonder. My hope is that you gain back some of the wonder that was taken away a long time ago.

While there is no magic wand that can undo the past, you *can* repaint your future—a future that is brighter than you could ever imagine. To paint that bright future, you have to turn on the lights. But before you do that, you must sit in the darkness, where thieves and monsters lurk, waiting to crush your wonder to steal the magic away. The cave you fear to enter holds the treasure you seek.[4]

Let's venture into the dark together.

CHAPTER 2

Wonder Switch Off

When Wonder Fades

My wonder was crushed by a man who recently died of anger, bitterness, and loneliness. The death certificate states that he died of natural causes, but a lot of hearts stop beating when they become bitter and broken.

I'm not sure why, but I was the sole executor and beneficiary of his will. The day he died, I was notified by a phone call while on tour. I was on a tour with six other speakers, authors, music artists, bands, and so on, speaking and performing for teenagers. Toward the end of the day at each event, all the speakers and performers held a Q & A session onstage based on questions submitted by the teens in attendance.

I remember standing in the hallway, listening to the voicemail on my phone.

"Harris, my name is Jim. We've never met, but I'm calling to let you know your friend has died. There's a will here stating you as the executor of his estate, as well as a letter talking about how much you meant to him, basically saying that you were the son he never had."

I did not know how to respond to this phone call. Emotions flooded to the surface. Emotions I hadn't felt in years. Before I had a chance to process this news, my tour manager came around the corner.

"Harris, it's almost time for Q & A."

"Where's Courtney?" I asked.

Courtney was the host of the event each weekend. It was also her job to take the questions submitted by the audience, and if they weren't directed to a specific speaker, she'd assign them to one of us. She walked around the corner, stack of questions in hand.

"Hey, do you mind answering this question?"

She handed me a slip of paper. It read, "How can I find the strength to forgive someone for something terrible they did to me?"

Immediately my heart raced, my skin became cold, and my palms grew sweaty—things I now understand as signs of unresolved trauma. I was entering dark spots of my story in the form of a flashback. My mind immediately went back to that moment.

"Take off your pants," he had said.

I was confused. I couldn't understand why that was necessary.

Even now, as I close my eyes and access the memory of that night somewhere in the outskirts of Columbus, I remember many details. I remember hearing those words, my heart rate accelerating, and immediately looking around the room, attempting not to make eye contact.

I remember the flickering pixels of the eighties TV playing in the background. I remember the musty smell of cheap cologne combined with the air freshener—like the smell of a just-cleaned, dingy motel room. I can recollect the sound of the heater murmuring in the corner of the room because I have a specific memory of looking at the green floral pattern of the curtains hanging in the window above it and ensuring that the curtains were closed. The same floral pattern was printed on the gross, scratchy comforters stretched across the beds.

I remember the giant black suitcase he always traveled with lying on the bed, filled with both clothing and magicians' gimmicks, and the way everything in it was meticulously labeled in little custom boxes, constantly leaving me to wonder if he was obsessive compulsive or a hoarder. I remember the silk handkerchiefs, the kind magicians perform tricks with, lying in piles on the bed, and some of the unboxed gimmicks.

As weird as this may seem, for me, it was just another normal night on the road. But nothing about that night ended up being normal.

We were at a magicians' conference, a sort of "underground" gathering of those fascinated by the art of magic and illusion. His name was Bill, or "Reverend Baker," as everyone called him, and he was one of my magic mentors. In this instance, we were on a lecture tour of a collection of conventions hosted by a particular niche brotherhood of illusionists and other variety performers.

A year or two before I met Bill, I had fallen in love with magic tricks and met my first mentor, Mr. McMichael. He was an amateur magician who performed in our local area. I had met him at the age of nine, shortly after I became fascinated with the idea of becoming a magician. I wouldn't trade my time with him or what he taught me for anything in the world. He was a kind, generous, and admirable man and was the catalyst for so much of the work I am doing even to this day. At the time, he had, in his words, taken me "as far as he could."

Mr. McMichael had introduced me to the first magic organization I became a member of, and as a result, I met many of those in leadership who taught at their conventions. Bill was the leader who most encouraged and affirmed my talent. He made me feel like a star every time he saw me.

Bill and I were a year or so into our relationship of teacher and student when I found myself in that dimly lit motel room in Ohio. I was excited to finish our day at the conference and get back to the room for my next private lesson. It was one I had been asking about and looking forward to since he had started teaching me.

The subject: dove magic. Yeah, I know—this story keeps getting weirder. I'm sure you've seen classic magicians make birds appear onstage from seemingly nowhere. A magician pulls out a colored handkerchief, displays it, then—*poof*—a dove.

As you can imagine, magicians hide stuff everywhere—behind curtains, inside trapdoors, between secret panels, in the palms of our hands, inside our jackets, and often, right in front of your face. And apparently, as I was about to learn, we also hide things in our pants.

"Take off your pants."

"Why?" I asked immediately.

"Well, you can only fit so many birds inside your jacket and sleeves, and a lot of guys also hide their pulls in their pants."

A "pull" is a magician's term for the action of taking whatever they're hiding and secretly transferring it to the position they need it in before making it visible to the audience. There's a reason why magicians are known for saying, "See? Nothing up my sleeves!" We love to keep things up our sleeves and secretly pull them out at the right moment—handkerchiefs, flowers, you name it. But a dove? In my pants? I didn't understand.

But Bill had a short temper. He was old and cranky and had a long history of moving around from place to place, and I desperately wanted to learn from him. After all, he *was* an amazing magician in his younger years. There was a rumor at the time that he had helped train one of the world's most successful magicians early in his career. Getting famous sounded amazing. At the time, I wanted nothing less than to be the next David Copperfield.

After more than a year of training and him investing in my life, his strange instruction came seemingly out of nowhere. Needless to say, I was a little freaked out. And thus began a period of about three years of strange and confusing experiences that I wouldn't understand until later in life to be child molestation.

When Innocence Dies

I lived a pretty sheltered life until the abuse started. I grew up in a small town on old farmland. Before I was abused, the evilest thing I remember being exposed to was the time someone broke into our home while we weren't there.

There was also one time when I stole a fake wedding ring from a bag of wedding cake decorations from my grandmother's bakery. I had a crush on a girl at school and thought she'd think I bought her jewelry. I don't remember how old I was, but I had obviously not hit puberty because my only desire was for her to "like me back." My imagination gave birth to no other desire. I suppose it also could have been that my imagination had yet to be hijacked and sexualized, even as a kid. As a child of the eighties, I didn't grow up with a computer or a cell phone, let alone an internet connection.

But a few years went by, and I found myself in that hotel room, trying to come to grips with the realities of what I could only assume to be the real world.

After it happened that first time, I lay in bed, pretending to be asleep, trying to make sense of the world and my place in it, while my abuser lay in the other bed, watching a late-night HBO film.

Then I realized how much more enjoyable it was to watch a girl take off her clothes and get naked on a TV screen than to take off mine in front of a creepy old man.

Then a friend of my parents built us an inexpensive computer around the same time AOL started sending us free CD-ROMs to try out this thing called the internet, a party my family was severely late to.

Then I realized you could search the internet for anything.

Then I wondered if the kind of HBO videos I watched at the hotel could be found on my computer.

Then I realized that instead of looking at pictures of adults, a more appealing idea was to find pictures of girls my age, the kind of girls I wanted to like me.

That didn't work at all. The first time I typed that search, AOL said, "Goodbye."

Imagine having that conversation with your dad. I had to imagine it for hours while waiting for my dad to come home from work.

"Dad, I got kicked off AOL, and they canceled our account." I rehearsed it in my head.

I had racked my brain all afternoon for a suitable lie I could tell him. I couldn't think of one, so I called AOL. Before I could even fabricate a story, they asked for additional information to verify my identity. I didn't know what to say, so I immediately hung up.

Minutes later, I was digging through the family filing cabinet in search of a credit card number, social security number, and any other info I might need to make another phone call. I dialed the toll-free number again for AOL. The wait for a real person on the line felt like an eternity.

"Thank you for calling AOL. How can I help you?"

"Um, we're having difficulties logging in to our account."

"What's your information, sir?"

I gave her my dad's full legal name and our address. In my mind, I wasn't lying. I'm a third, which means my dad and I have the same name.

"Can I get your social security number for security purposes?"

I read it off to her. (Now I was officially lying.)

"Sir, it looks like our company terminated your account for violating our policy regarding underage pornography."

"I'm sorry?"

"Yes, sir. It appears as though someone in your family searched for nude photos of girls under the age of eighteen."

"I wasn't even on the computer earlier this afternoon," I blurted.

"Could there have been a friend or other family member using your computer, sir?"

"I don't think so."

"I'm sorry, Mr. Harris, but we have very strict policies regarding this kind of subject matter, and unfortunately there's nothing we can do to reactivate your account. It has been permanently terminated. We have very clear records of what was searched for."

"It must have been my son. I'm sure he didn't understand what he was doing, or that his actions were illegal and against the law," I said, doing my best to talk with a deep voice to sound older.

"Again, I'm sorry, sir, but there's nothing I can do."

I hung up the phone.

"I'm dead."

I had a long talk with my dad that afternoon after *he* called AOL and had what was probably a repeat of the conversation I had with them earlier. I tried to pretend like I had no idea why our account was terminated, thinking maybe, just maybe, he wouldn't call to find out why. Yeah, that was stupid.

And yet even during pornography-driven conversations with my dad about sex, I still didn't tell him about being sexually abused. I just sat on the floor with my face buried in nervous, sweaty palms, crying confused tears of shame. Shame I still feel, even though I was just a kid.

The American Psychological Association states, "The strongest indication that a child has been sexually abused is inappropriate sexual knowledge, sexual interest, and sexual acting out by that child."[1] We repeat what we don't repair. As children, we try to make sense of the stories we found ourselves in through play and exploration.

My innocence was murdered, and its death led to newfound sexual knowledge, which spurred interest and curiosity in things a child wasn't ready to explore. It all led to a pornography addiction, a secret I thought I could keep to myself. And I justified it all by thinking, "At least I'm not drinking, doing meth, and sleeping around like the rest of the kids in my school."

Isn't it amazing how we justify our actions by comparing ourselves with others? It's easy to find faults in others so that we can feel better about our own brokenness. After all, it's easier to believe a lie than it is to face the truth. It's no surprise that we often ignore wonder. If we stop lying, the truth is no longer hidden in the corner of a dark room. The day I found out about Bill's death, I was about to tell my truth.

Some Secrets Aren't Meant to Be Kept

Courtney had handed me that slip of paper with this question: "How can I find the strength to forgive someone for something terrible they did to me?"

"Harris, will you answer this question?" Courtney asked me.

"Um, sure?" was all I could muster. I had no idea why I agreed to answer this question. I must have been in shock.

Moments later, I found myself onstage telling three thousand teenagers about being molested as a child. Sadly, in that moment I didn't have much wisdom to share about how forgiveness works, but something special happened onstage that day. I told the truth about something terrible someone had done to me. As I stood there onstage, microphone in hand, I forgave him.

At least I said I did. I even thought I did.

If I'm honest, I tried. At the time, I had always heard the saying "Forgive and forget." But how could I possibly forget?

I've since learned that forgiveness didn't mean excusing what he had done to hurt me. It didn't mean putting an end to the feelings that had come rushing back to the surface or that I was vowing to simply forget that something had ever happened. In some small way, sharing my story was just the first step—the beginning of a long journey toward wholeness and the hope of a new chapter in my story.

This all may be difficult to believe, but on that day, I learned that forgiveness was the first step toward healing and letting go. The forgiveness wasn't for his story—it was for mine. It was an acceptance of the reality that I had tried so hard for so long to forget, which caused the pain from that trauma to be suppressed and pushed below the surface, out of my conscious thought. But it was always there, waiting to be dealt with.

When I walked offstage at the end of the event, thankfully, a man I admired named Max Lucado stood in the hallway. He met me with a warm smile filled with empathy. He was the first person to provide a little counsel while I dealt with an onslaught of unfamiliar emotions.

After our conversation backstage, it became evident to me that the night had been divinely orchestrated. That entire afternoon and evening was exactly what I needed in those moments. Lies and illusions had wreaked their havoc, but that night, real magic was at work.

Think about it: an old magician teaching a kid about tricks as a means of tricking him into thinking that something is okay—it is "not what it seems." Then he keeps everything a secret and encourages him to do the same because "others would misunderstand."

Sometimes the greatest illusions we create are the ones we live offstage.

Two months after Bill's death, I felt ready to make the trip to his home in Florida. His belongings consisted mainly of a few boxes of books, a few personal items, and a suitcase of old props—the same suitcase that sat on the bed of that hotel room in Columbus twenty years before. It's hard to put into words what I felt picking up that suitcase and loading it into the trunk of my car.

When my wife and I got back home to Nashville, we sat down together to unpack the suitcase. Both of us were unaware of the secrets we would discover by digging through the history of his life. We found letters hidden inside secret compartments hidden in books, written by other boys. The scene sounds like the stuff of movies, but the compartments and the letters were real. The letters contained content that made me want to vomit.

Within twenty-four hours, I had connected dots and tracked down others, having conversations by phone with multiple magicians, young and old, who shared my same experiences of molestation, many times with familiar stories and details. The ones in the magic industry were easier to contact because of shared relationships. The ones I couldn't track down but later became aware of were the dozens of boys pictured in troop photos in Boy Scout scrapbooks and the many kids of church groups he helped lead during his years as a religious leader at a church.

After more research and conversations, I learned how this man had resigned from multiple churches because of accusations of molestation that were never fully proved. The deeper I dug, the more I found. And the more I found, the angrier and more depressed I became. The forgiveness I had offered publicly onstage only a few weeks before was now slipping through my fingers.

How could someone do this? My experiences as a kid had led me to think for the longest time that this guy was a creepy old man who obviously had some mental issues. Sure, it was weird. He was weird. And aren't we all a little weird? But a child molester? It took me years to see the truth.

As the truth dawned on me, it was like the secret of a magic trick being revealed. When you're first exposed to magic, you know you're being deceived, but you can't figure out the secret to the trick, so you spend the whole time in the dark, wondering what the truth is. Then suddenly, you catch a glimpse of the hidden thread in the light, or the magician's sleight of hand isn't as smooth as it should have been, and the truth hits you. "Ah. So that's what's going on."

That week, everything made sense. He wasn't just "weird," as I had labeled him in my naive, childlike, innocent mind. He really was a child molester. But as a child, I was unable to process what happened to me in a way that would allow me to see the whole truth. I still carried around the baggage of the first ten years of my childhood, and the belief systems that decade had formed affected my ability to see clearly. Going through his personal items revealed far more than I ever expected. It revealed the secret to a trick I never wanted to learn. But like all truth, in a strange and unexpected way, it led to freedom.

If the truth can set us free, that must mean lies can entangle us. Unfortunately, we don't often gain the perspective that allows us to see the lies we've been seduced into believing until we've already been trapped. With new context for my abuse, I realized that the lies we believe lead us to tell untrue stories to ourselves.

Now I'm able to see that the day I took off my pants in that hotel room, I put on a straitjacket, a metaphorical reality of the physical straitjackets and chains I had been professionally trained to escape. My identity began to be reshaped, the way I viewed myself morphed and changed, and with each lie, another strap of my straitjacket was tightened. The web of lies entangled my life, and the truth that would set me free was long from being discovered. My wonder was crushed, and I was confused in the darkness, struggling to hold on to hope.

Many nights at his house in Florida—during times I would go to learn more magic—I would go to bed trying to stay silent as I cried myself to sleep because I was so confused. Crying yourself to sleep every night in isolation doesn't make for a confident, healthy boy desperate to begin his journey to becoming a man.

But I kept it a secret. I didn't understand what was going on, and I was scared to death of what others might think. All I could think was, "What if my parents find out? I won't be able to come here anymore and learn everything I've been learning. And not only that, I'll get in trouble too because I'm sure this is my fault because I let it happen. And maybe he's right . . . maybe it really is nothing, and others would misunderstand it to be something it's not."

So many lies.

Research shows that a lot of the psychological damage experienced by someone who has been sexually abused is not only from the assault itself but from the post-abuse reactions from others. I didn't know about that research or about the science that shows how we freeze in fear as our central nervous system attempts to integrate the experience of sexual abuse. But somehow, deep down, I knew enough to fear how others would react. My desire to please others and maintain my image, especially as I became a young teenager, pressured me to keep everything just as secret as the explanations to my tricks. Magicians are really good at keeping secrets. Of course, some secrets aren't meant to be kept, but like all children who experience this and other kinds of trauma, I didn't have the words or language to explain what was happening. The part of our brain that is responsible for language production is shut down when we are experiencing trauma. Literally, there were no thoughts, feelings, or words capable of being shared.

The greatest irony of my story may be that the man who was responsible for teaching me how to perform tricks onstage played a trick on me and, in turn, stole my belief in magic.

The Mind of a Child

We are all born awake to wonder. But then we are lulled to sleep. We are bullied. We are lied to. We're abused. We are told to "grow up." We're yelled at or treated unfairly by a grown-up. Sometimes our mentors molest us. And the wonder of our childhood is crushed.

Wonder switch off.

See, this is my opinion: we all start out knowing magic. We are born with whirlwinds, forest fires, and comets inside us. We are born able to sing to birds and read the clouds and see our destiny in grains of sand. But then we get the magic educated right out of our souls. We get it churched out, spanked out, washed out, and combed out. We get put on the straight and narrow and told to be responsible. Told to act our age. Told to grow up, for God's sake. And you know why we were told that? Because the people doing the telling were afraid of our wildness and youth, and because the magic we knew made them ashamed and sad of what they'd allowed to wither in themselves.

After you go so far away from it, though, you can't really get it back. You can have seconds of it. Just seconds of knowing and remembering. When people get weepy at movies, it's because in that dark theater the golden pool of magic is touched, just briefly. Then they come out into the hard sun of logic and reason again and it dries up, and they're left feeling a little heartsad and not knowing why. When a song stirs at memory, when motes of dust turning in a shaft of light takes your attention from the world, when you listen to a train passing on a track at night in the distance and wonder where it might be going, you step beyond who you are and where you are. For the briefest of instants, you have stepped into the magic realm. That's what I believe.[2]

I love that passage from the opening of the novel *Boy's Life* by Robert R. McCammon. I believe those things too. It should come as no surprise that this novel exists in a genre labeled as "fantasy."

You came into this world believing in magic, believing anything was possible. What crushed your wonder? When wonder fades, our ability to dream big fades with it. We do as we're told by the world around us. We settle for the status quo—counterfeit versions of the lives we're capable of living. We certainly don't attempt the extraordinary, like sending people into space to explore the universe, in an attempt to explore who we are. We don't even look up and marvel at the stars, because we're far too busy looking down at our phones.

But what if there were a switch? A switch that, if turned back on, could help you reclaim the innocence of your childhood? A kind of wonder that, if truly reawakened, could change everything about how you see? A switch that gave you permission to believe in all the possibilities that await you?

That switch is real, and we now have the neuroscience to back it up. It's the wonder switch. And leaving the wonder switch off is killing us. Our inability to stand wide awake in wonder of the magic around us, and the magic inside us, literally wages war on our bodies and lives.

That war started when you were tricked into trading the truth for a lie. When the wonder of your childhood died, and your innocence died with it. When the magic was educated right out of your soul.

But what is magic, really? Is it found in the sleight of hand of a card trick or the artful execution of a supposedly death-defying escape? The spectacle of a lady getting cut in half and put back together again, or watching her mysteriously levitate in the air?

Those are the thoughts many people conjure up in their minds when they hear the word *magic*. And if I perform any of those seemingly impossible feats onstage, people refer to me as a magician, but to me, those aren't examples of magic at all—those are just clever illusions.

Magic isn't something you can watch someone perform on a stage; it's what you feel in response to an experience that you can't quite put into words. When you witness something that seems impossible, the awe that wells up inside you that sparks wonder—that childlike feeling—that's magic. And we were all meant to experience lives filled with real magic—the extraordinary that exists all around us in the seemingly ordinary, often right in front of our eyes.

I can only perform illusions on stage. But what if magic is real, and what if you could experience it daily? Again, I'm not talking about the fake stuff like the tricks I do. I'm talking about real magic. A life filled with love, hope, joy, belonging, faith, meaning, purpose—experiences that transcend what you can see with your eyes. I've discovered that a lot of people don't believe that kind of life is possible, but being an illusionist has taught me that things aren't always as they seem.

What if there was a life of magic you were meant to experience, but you're settling for an illusion instead? Really think about it. So much of our society conspires against wonder, and when wonder is crushed and replaced with cynicism and lies, you live a counterfeit version of your life instead of the one you were meant to live. What if?

Wonder *can* be reawakened. When the wonder switch flips on, it has the power to change everything. The wonder switch changed my perspective, and then my life, and it can change yours too. Let's explore the untrue stories you're telling yourself and see if we can't right them along the way. If so, we can help you return to the magical life you've dreamed of living—the way you dreamed it as a child.

CHAPTER 3

The Old Story

Revisiting Your Past to
Discover Your Future

What is your first memory of experiencing wonder?

The first one I remember was when I was nine years old. I think it probably goes without saying that I'd already had experiences of wonder well before the age of nine. Hundreds of them, at least. You likely did too. And most of us can probably remember some of the experiences that wonder gave birth to—the stories we acted out, the monsters we fought, the bad guys we destroyed with the power of our imagination.

Wonder is the feeling you had when something welled up deep inside you and you whispered, "Maybe more is possible than I thought." The first experience of wonder that I remember happened a few days after Christmas.

Magic for Christmas

At the time, I was growing up in southeast Tennessee in a town called Evensville, home at the time to just over a thousand people. My dad worked at a factory in the area, spending all day cutting out foam that went inside furniture. My mom was a housekeeper at a small college. When your parents have near–minimum wage jobs, it's hard to be one of the cool kids. And by fourth grade, I struggled to find a way to fit in and belong.

We lived in the middle of nowhere, so in elementary school, kids never came to play at my house. Not that I really wanted them to. By that time I was embarrassed by the Mickey Mouse wallpaper I'd picked out for my room during kindergarten.

It wasn't that I didn't have any friends at school; I just didn't feel known. I didn't feel like I fit in. I was bullied a lot and made fun of often as I attempted to find my place and figure out who I was. To make matters worse, a new kid had moved to our little town that year and brought with him an attitude and behavior that pervaded our innocent, rural fourth-grade class of about a dozen kids.

It wasn't only me who didn't see possibility anywhere. My family was in the lower part of the "middle class" of the rural South. Dreaming just wasn't part of our culture, except for the hope we placed in winning the lottery. But soon everything would change. I was about to receive magic for Christmas, and I never saw it coming.

The year I turned nine also happened to be the year I was obsessed with baseball. Not because I was good at it by any stretch, but I had found an old glove in one of the barns on my great-grandparents' property, which was connected to ours. It was worn out and didn't fit well. So I did what any kid would have done. I asked for a new one for Christmas.

All I wanted for Christmas that year was a brand-new baseball glove. I remember going to Walmart's sports section during each visit, trying on all the gloves, picking out the perfect one, and telling every single member of our family which one it was that I wanted. Christmas morning finally came, we opened our gifts, and there was no glove. Yet. There was still hope: Grandma and Grandpa's house.

My dad was originally from St. Louis, Missouri. He moved to our little town to go to college after his years in the Air Force. My mom was now a housekeeper at that same college. After he met my mom and married her, I came along about a year later, and he traded his dream for a job at the local La-Z-Boy factory, out of what I'm sure felt like the necessity to provide for his new family. But my grandparents? They still lived in St. Louis, and that year, we were headed their way a few days after Christmas.

As soon as we arrived at their house, I still remember jumping out of the car to run inside. It was well after midnight. I checked under their Christmas tree, and I spotted it. A box, with my name on it, that was the perfect size to hold the glove I'd asked for. With my desire for that glove fully satisfied, I remember being fine with my Grandma saying, "Nuh-uh-uh! We'll open presents tomorrow morning."

The next morning, I opened that perfectly sized box with gusto, only to have my high hopes instantly gutted. It wasn't a baseball glove after all. To make things even worse, it was a box of magic tricks. My immediate thought? "This is stupid." What's crazy is that I received a slew of other presents that year, and to this day, that's the only gift I remember—the one I never even wanted. But life has a way of working like that. Often we don't get what we want but, in its place, receive exactly what we need. Real magic is at work.

It took a few days before I was either finally curious enough or, more likely, just bored. But eventually I opened that little box of tricks and learned my first illusion. It was called the ball and vase trick. Apparently, you could take a little red ball and put it inside a little vase, cover it with the lid, and make the ball "disappear."

All I could think in that moment was, "This is dumb. No one is going to be fooled by this." And to prove I was right, I went to perform for my first audience. I walked into the living room. Mom and Dad were watching TV. With an eye roll and a dose of nine-year-old sarcasm, I announced, "Mom and Dad, gather around! Here's what Grandma got me for Christmas."

I put the ball in the cup. It disappeared. I put the lid back on; the ball reappeared. It was a simple trick. But what did my parents say?

Nothing, at first. They were speechless.

As their eyes widened, their chins dropped. Finally, they said what I would eventually go on to hear thousands of people say over the course of my career.

"Whoa. How did you do that!"

"I'm sorry?" I said. This was not at all the response I expected. I was totally confused.

"How did you do that? That was amazing!" Their eyes lit up with wonder.

It was the first time I remember someone viewing me with a look of awe in their eyes in response to something I had done. Immediately, magic was cool, and I thought I might perform it for the rest of my life. I was hooked. Wonder began to work its magical power.

Wonder switch on.

The Birth of Possibility

I didn't realize it at the time, but that contagious experience of wonder with my parents turned my wonder switch on and began to change what I could see.

In the days that followed, we would eventually pack up our stuff and drive back to southeast rural Tennessee, but this time I wasn't going home with only a few Christmas gifts in tow—I was going home with a dream. Wonder gave birth to that dream, and I was still naive enough to believe it might be possible.

When wonder is reawakened, you begin to see opportunity everywhere. My newfound wonder gave birth to a whole new story of possibility.

The whole trip back home to Tennessee, sitting in the back seat of my parents' old Subaru, I stared out the window like I always had. Previous trips were spent practically banging my head against that window out of boredom, asking my parents, "Are we there yet?" I had spent those trips daydreaming in an effort to escape the small-town life I'd been living. But this time the visions were different. It was as if all the other trips on that same route were through a completely different landscape.

I was no longer daydreaming about running away from something. I'd found a dream that felt worthy of pursuit, and wonder had gifted me with the belief that the dream might be possible. I had all sorts of visions of stardom, most of which were variations of gracing stages, receiving applause, and getting rich and famous traveling the world as a magician.

In the short time that followed, I mastered all the tricks in that first magic kit my grandmother had given me for Christmas. The next year, a magician showed up in my town and performed tricks for the kids at the church my parents dragged me to each Sunday. I begged him to teach me some "professional" tricks, and he agreed. His name was David McMichael, and he was the amazing first mentor I told you about earlier.

It wasn't long before I was performing magic at birthday parties, family reunions, church gatherings, nursing homes, and for anyone else who would let me put on a show. My bookings grew, and so did my confidence, along with my ego. I was featured at industry gatherings and magician conferences. I entered national competitions, won some trophies, garnered some attention from professionals, and successfully added "award-winning" to my résumé. And then I met Bill, the mentor who I was sure would lead me to stardom.

I never became famous, at least not outside of my small hometown, but I did feel rich. And I was able to live my dream of traveling the world. By the time I was fourteen years old, I dropped out of public school to tour full-time. I had already experienced the abuse of my childhood a few years earlier but had buried it and moved on. At least I thought I had. I told myself it was time to "grow up" and make a living, and everything in the world around me told me the same.

By sixteen years old, I made well into six figures each year performing magic shows. I performed anywhere people would let me, from schools to church buildings to private parties to even cruise ships in the Caribbean. By eighteen, I'd been booked in almost all fifty states and started doing shows in Europe and Asia.

All because of the gift I never wanted.

By the time I was twenty-one, I'd married my wife, Kate, the woman of my dreams, and we proceeded to tour the world, performing magic shows together. I'd also made a million dollars performing those magic shows by that time, and with it, purchased the American dream. I moved out of that small town, and we built a big house in a wealthy suburb of Nashville, parked two nice cars in the driveway, and even had one of those white picket fences around it all, just like in the movies.

We filled our house with expensive leather furniture and big screen TVs, and we even had a big walk-in closet for all my overpriced jeans. From the outside looking in, life was pretty awesome. So it seemed. But I had yet to be an illusionist long enough to learn that things aren't always as they seem.

Over the course of twelve short months, I would come to the realization that the illusionist, the supposed "expert" in the art of deception, somewhere along the way had been cleverly tricked and deceived. But at that point, I couldn't sit back and blame everyone else for deceiving me. I was also deceiving myself.

By twenty-two, I was bankrupt. I was stressed. I worked nonstop to solve all the problems I'd brought on through financial recklessness, often working well through dinners and into long nights. I started feeling more shame. I started withdrawing from relationships. My new marriage started struggling. And eventually I hit rock bottom. My wonder switch was definitely off. I'm not sure it had been turned back on since Bill had taken a sledgehammer and crushed it that night in a hotel room in Ohio. But I guess somewhere along the way, I had heard that some people fake it until they make it, and becoming a magician had made me really good at faking it. In our current culture, "putting on a show," whether on stage or off, is regularly rewarded.

Eventually, I discovered that I wasn't rich after all. Sure, I'd made a million dollars before most people graduate from college, but some people are so poor, all they have is money. And I was still so busy trying to become famous—not only by keeping up with the Joneses but by trying to outperform them—that I'd taken all my money and spent it. Every penny I had and then some.

As we discovered in the first chapter of this book, not all the stories we tell ourselves are true.

Straitjackets, Razor Blades, and the Most Powerful People in the World

Not long after making a million dollars and wasting it, my wife and I ended up selling everything we owned. We sold so much stuff that we felt like all we had left was each other. We moved to the opposite side of our city to a much cheaper, older section of town that had far less veneer. I kept performing magic but didn't have much clarity around my career as a magician. I kept saying yes to invitations to perform, if anything, to keep making good money so I could dig out of a mountain of debt.

For one of those performances, I was in a small town in Michigan, doing a show at a public high school. I leaned up against the side wall of the school's gym as hundreds of students walked in, finding seats in the bleachers above. I wished I were somewhere else. I was only there to promote the real show I was going to do later that night in a theater down the street. There isn't a professional entertainer anywhere in America who gets excited about performing in a high school gymnasium with a crappy sound system, down on the gym floor with no stage, with rowdy students peering down from their seats on squeaky bleachers.

Just before it was time to begin the show, the principal walked in.

"Are you the magician?"

"Yes, sir."

"You know how to trick people, right?"

"I suppose so. That's why you hired me, right?" I said with a wink and a nod.

"Then why don't you go out there and do some show-and-tell? Teach those kids how they're getting tricked into making the choices they're making."

Before I could finish my "Ummm . . ." he was out there introducing me to the audience.

I didn't know what to do in that situation. I went out and did the tricks I planned on performing, and I don't remember much about what I said. I remember finishing with a straitjacket escape and saying something about what I was experiencing in my own life: how lies can trap and entangle you but that the truth can set you free. I said something like, "I don't know what your straitjacket is, but I want you to know that if you're struggling with something that you can't seem to find freedom from, there's always hope."

While I don't remember much about that show itself, I will never forget what happened when it ended, for it would go on to cue one of my life's greatest epiphanies and serve as the catalyst for the meaningful work I'm still doing today.

As soon as I ended, all the students got up to leave, except for one girl. She sat there in her spot in the bleachers, looking down at me with tears in her eyes, eventually getting up and walking toward me. I didn't know what was happening. I'd never had anyone do that after a show before.

She walked up to me and said, "I have something for you."

"Um, okay. What is it?"

"Hold out your hands."

She reached into her pocket, held her hand over mine, and

dropped a small razor blade into my hands and said, "That's my straitjacket, and I don't want it anymore. No one has ever made me feel like there might be hope like you did today. Thank you."

A teacher came around the corner, gathering straggling students, and said, "Time to go back to class."

I never got that girl's name. But as she turned and walked away and put her hands into her pockets, I'll never forget seeing glimpses of her wrists and the scars that extended from under the sleeves of her hoodie.

All I could think was, "Why would someone do that to themselves?" I don't know what story she had lived up until that point, but I became curious what led to that place of self-harm. The more I thought of that girl, the more I became obsessed with answering that question: Why?

So I set off on a mission to understand why. Continuing with the entertainment business as usual didn't just no longer feel exciting—it didn't even feel like an option. I had gotten a glimpse of purpose, of stage magic that could return people to *real* magic, and I wanted more.

That principal had encouraged me to "show the students" something about themselves. The only thing I was there to show them was how great I was at magic so they would choose to come to an even better show that night at their local theater. But maybe he was on to something, seeing a creative possibility that I had yet to see myself. My wonder was sparked.

In my drive to understand for the sake of finding greater purpose, I eventually discovered the power of advertising and the influential role it plays in developing our identities and self-image. It wasn't hard to see that the era of advertising both that girl and I had grown up in was rooted in making others feel like they weren't enough without the right brand of clothes or right kind of car. If only we could be *seen*—seen driving that kind of car, wearing those kinds of clothes, hanging out with people living in certain parts of town. Well, *then* we'd be enough.

Most studies now show that the average American takes in about five thousand messages a day. Some digital marketers claim as many as ten thousand messages per day, a good number of which are advertisements.[1] Ninety percent of all the data in the world has been created in the last two years alone.[2] How much data did someone who lived in the 1800s consume? I have no idea—but probably not much, right? We live in such a media-saturated society that we now take in more information in an average day than the average human who lived a hundred years ago probably took in over the course of their entire lifetime. Pause and let that sink in.

What are all these stories telling us? And what are they doing to our wonder?

One of the primary narratives of all the messaging is some version of "I am not enough." We're subtly told as stories unfold that we aren't thin enough, rich enough, cool enough, talented enough, strong enough, pretty enough, handsome enough—just not enough. The list goes on and on. But wait! If only you had one of *these*! says the commercial. *Then* you would be enough. *Then* you'd be worthy of love and acceptance and belonging. But if you don't look like this, aren't seen with these kinds of people, don't live in this part of town, or don't drive this car around? Well, good luck.

The irony is that a subtle undertone of this multibillion-dollar advertising industry says, "Be yourself!" Only to be consistently followed up with, "No, not like that!" No wonder our wonder is struggling to stay alive. It's as if the world asks us who we are, and just when we're about to answer, we're shushed and told, "Be this instead."

Story-driven messaging is incredibly effective because, as psychology writer Jonathan Gottschall says in his insightful book *The Storytelling Animal*, humans are storytelling creatures who "live in landscapes of make-believe."[3] We don't just tell stories; we storify everything around us. We are neurologically hardwired for story.

Storytelling starts with the frontal cortex, a dominant part of our brain where "higher order" functions take place, like solving problems, making plans and decisions, and even engaging the imagination. The dominant part of our brain uses story as its operating system. Even now, we are thinking in "story." And to make sense of the world around us, we walk around all day telling ourselves stories. In fact, we are such storytelling creatures that when we climb into bed at night, our bodies physically sleep while our brains stay up all night long telling us more stories, filtering and filing our daily stories into the narrative of our life.

It should come as no surprise, then, that the stories we're told, whether by teachers and parents or marketers and advertisers, all shape the stories we tell ourselves. We take all the stories we're told and form a narrative because we try to make sense of the strange experiences and weird situations we find ourselves in. Story is a tool for survival.

It is survival, according to Gottschall, that drives the stories we tell ourselves and, therefore, all human behavior. "Stories universally focus on the great predicaments of the human condition," he writes. "The problem structure of story reveals a major function of storytelling. It suggests that the human mind was shaped *for* story, so that it could be shaped *by* story."[4]

Keith Oatley, professor emeritus of cognitive psychology at the University of Toronto, and a novelist, makes a great case that we love fiction because it serves as the flight simulator of our social lives.[5] If we fear abandonment, stories teach us how to survive by showing us how to interact with others and avoid being kicked out of our tribes.

Imagine for a moment that someone cuts you off in traffic. What keeps you from spiraling into a state of rage and running the person off the road? Scientists argue that the very thing that helps you stay rational is the fictional story you tell yourself. Your subconscious mind kicks into overdrive and rapidly plays out the fictional story that answers the question "What happens next?"

What happens next—your storytelling mind determines—may be that you end up in the ditch with the other car, possibly injuring you and anyone else in the car. Or maybe you would get pulled over by the police, be arrested, go to jail, and become an embarrassment to your family. Or at the very least, you would mess up your car, leaving a mark of your bad decision for all to see. Through the creation of this imaginary work of fiction, your brain decides it doesn't like the way that story ends, and so you therefore choose to swallow your pride and merely resort to name-calling, letting the person who wronged you drive away and go about their day.

This may sound crazy to you simply because you can't remember the last time you played the story out in your head. But that's because this all takes place below the level of conscious awareness. Story lives in the instinctual part of our brains.

Gottschall echoes Oatley by writing,

Like a flight simulator, fiction projects us into intense simulations of problems that run parallel to those we face in reality.

And like a flight simulator, the main virtue of fiction is that we have a rich experience and don't die at the end. We get to simulate what it would be like to confront a dangerous man or seduce someone's spouse, for instance, and the hero of the story dies in our stead. So, this line of reasoning goes, we seek story because we enjoy it. But nature designed us to enjoy stories so we would get the benefit of practice. Fiction is an ancient virtual reality technology that specializes in simulating human problems.[6]

In other words, we don't just choose to tell ourselves stories—we *must* tell ourselves stories to survive. In our modern era, survival is no longer needing the safety of a tribe so we aren't eaten by a lion. Instead, we need a tribe so that our sense of belonging outweighs being wounded by the words of a parent, a bully at school, a jerk at work, or the trolls who seem to pervade online comment sections. We need a tribe to counterbalance the negativity we receive and help us "survive" the one-star reviews from strangers in response to our work.

When these kinds of things trigger our survival instincts, our brains immediately go to work to explain the situation. "Why did that person do that? Why did he say that? Is it true? Do I really suck and should just throw in the towel?" Studies like Kuleshov's experiment show that our brain can't avoid telling us a story to make sense of and find patterns and meaning in seemingly random things.[7]

This explains, for example, how the real story "Once upon a time, my mom asked me why I didn't take better care of myself and told me to watch my weight" leads to the lie "I am fat." That lie causes pain, and our mind strives to make sense of that pain. That pain was also an unanticipated part of our story, which introduces the question all stories ask: What happens next? The attempt to find meaning in this part of our story, and answer that question in an effort to inform future behavior, gives birth to a work of fiction: "I am ugly, and I'm going to be single and all alone forever."

But we don't want to be alone forever. And so those who sell jeans or cars or makeup tap into this deep longing for belonging—something neuroscientists call "character identification." Neuroimaging shows that our brains empathize with, relate to, and even mimic characters in a story (or advertisement), as if we actually undergo what the character experiences.

It should come as no surprise, then, that marketers use advertisements to tell stories that associate products we *don't* truly need for survival with the connection and belonging we *do* need. As marketing guru Seth Godin says, "People do not buy goods and services. They buy relations, stories, and magic."[8]

In one of my favorites of Godin's writings, he uses the example of a diamond ring. He writes, "Walk through the diamond district in Manhattan and in the course of one block, at least a dozen men will stop you and ask if you're hoping to sell a diamond ring. A few blocks away, Tiffany will happily sell you a diamond ring. Buy a $7,000 ring at Tiffany's and walk over to one of these guys and you'll be lucky to get $1,000 for your new ring."[9]

What's the reason for the difference in cost? As Godin beautifully explains, "That $6,000 is what you paid for the story." The story of a small blue box.

A car isn't an engine-powered metal frame that transports you from one place to another; it's often promoted as a powerful tool that can change the way others look at you and even how you see yourself when you look in the mirror. Car manufacturers don't really try to sell you a car—they try to sell you a story.

Jeans aren't just jeans. Shoes aren't just shoes. Makeup isn't just makeup. If it were, most ads would describe a product's quality and features, not just show images of photoshopped models, right? And if perfume or cologne were marketed as scented liquid that you can spray on yourself to make you smell better, would the cost be anywhere near what it's often sold for? How much is scented alcohol and water per ounce? A lot less than cologne that makes a woman stop in her tracks and look at me like *that* woman did in the commercial.

But what if we don't buy the right jeans, wear the right makeup, have the right waist size, or belong to the right "tribe"? We experience pain. And sadly, many harm themselves in an effort to forget about the pain others caused. The narrative is broken.

When we buy lies over truth, we're settling for what seems to be the new "reality." Not because it is reality but because the fiction *feels* like reality. Counterfeits can seem so real. It's not that we're dense; marketing stories are meticulously *designed* to seem real. The scripts are written by marketing pros from high-rise advertising agencies who know what they're doing. So we end up settling for counterfeit versions of the lives we were meant to live, instead of lives filled with real magic. You may have settled for a counterfeit version of your life because the crushing of your wonder permitted you to buy the lie or because the buying of the lies, over time, crushed your wonder. The reason varies from story to story, from person to person. You are a complex storytelling creature, and if wonder is a switch, then stories are the electricity that feeds that switch.

One of wonder's greatest powers is that it changes the stories we tell ourselves. It can change the narrative that drives all our choices and behavior.

Perhaps this is why in 1994 Steve Jobs, in a break room conversation at NeXT, while making a bagel, quipped, "The most powerful person in the world is the storyteller. The storyteller sets the vision, values, and agenda of an entire generation that is to come."[10] That was the same Steve Jobs who, with his team at Apple, created the device on which many of you are reading or listening to this book and the device on which many of you ordered your copy of this book. And the device on which I am writing this book.

Steve Jobs understood the power of stories. But the iPhone didn't experience explosive success in the marketplace just because it gave us greater access to the stories we wanted to be told, or because of how we find ourselves in those stories. Its success was unprecedented because it provided us the tools to tell the stories we feel the need to tell.

Putting On a Show

Remember when you were praised for everything? There was probably a time in your childhood when you received applause for peeing in a toilet instead of your diaper. People clapped for you and sang your praises for the most basic human achievements.

You were more than enough. You had it all.

Until one day the clapping stopped.

You were more than enough.

Until you weren't.

You found yourself broken and hurting.

Then came the lie: "I am not enough."

That was a lie I believed, but who wrote that script and put it in my hands? A lot of people over the course of my life. But it was first handed to me by the bullies on the playground at school. They crushed my wonder, but my parents reawakened it when I performed that first feat of "magic," crushing that lie and permitting me to embrace my human potential.

And then came my abuser, trying to take control of the narrative, crushing my wonder again, and permitting the lie to be echoed by others throughout my teen years. The lie was then reinforced by tens of thousands of ads trying to sell me a way out of my shame. Ads that said, "You *could* be enough, if only you could be seen driving this kind of car, wearing these kinds of clothes, living in this kind of house, hanging out with these kinds of people. If only you belonged."

It took me a long time to realize that I didn't buy expensive cars and clothes because I was selfish. I didn't build a house at twenty-one years old because I was materialistic and cared only about nice things. I bought that stuff for the same reason many others do—because I did everything in my power to show the world that I was enough, that I had what it took. I wanted my friends and family to drive down my street and say, "Look at him now." I thought if I could get them to "look at me now," then they might accept me because they liked what they saw. And if they could accept me, then maybe I could accept myself.

My vocation as an illusionist became my lifestyle. I would walk onstage, do a show, and receive applause. But when I walked offstage, I didn't want the show to end, and I didn't want the applause to end either. Every round of applause, onstage or off—in the form of a like on Instagram or a compliment from a friend—served as an affirmation that I was enough, or more clearly, as a confirmation of the story I wanted to be true.

You may never set foot on a stage or be in a spotlight, but many of us are still putting on one heck of a show. The phones in our pockets have given us access to stages with bigger audiences than could ever fit into a single theater. Scientists now link the dopamine that floods our brains when we see likes on our social media posts to the hit the human brain receives from addictive narcotics like cocaine.

Why are we performing? Are we comparing ourselves with others, trying to measure up? As Jon Acuff says, we compare our behind-the-scenes with everyone else's highlight reel. But why do we compare the movie of our life story with those of others? Or as my friend Marc Pimsler once told me in a conversation about the role of shame, "We compare our insides to other people's outsides."

Perhaps we aren't comparing ourselves to others as much as we are comparing the story we wish to be living against the one we're telling ourselves about who we are. In other words, what feels like a comparison to others is actually a comparison to one's ideal self. Where does your ideal self come from? And is it the truest version of yourself? Or is it rooted in lies and illusions?

It is easy to be deceived and even easier to deceive ourselves. The principles of deception that make magic tricks possible are universal. When I was a kid, I was taught *how* magic tricks work. As I got older and started understanding the power of story, I began to care about *why* magic tricks work. I discovered that an illusionist's ability to trick you is directly connected to your willingness to submit to the story they lead you to think you're experiencing, leading you to tell yourself a story that isn't true. Illusionists don't need to lie to trick people. Basically, illusionists create scenarios in which people deceive themselves.

Can we trust our senses? Is seeing really believing? Maybe what we perceive to be true with our senses and feelings is not always reality. It might be time to check the narrative ruling your life and driving your choices and behavior, because the story you're telling yourself shapes the story you're living. That untrue story you were fed is what turned your wonder switch off, and it stays off by repeating that story over and over again.

It's time to change the narrative.

By now I hope you're beginning to understand that the same thing that is crushing your wonder today is most likely the thing that crushed your wonder as a child. Most psychologists agree that most of what shapes your current belief systems was in place by the time you were seven years old.

Maybe the thought of facing rejection or failure has paralyzed you. Perhaps you can acknowledge that fear hijacks situations, bossing you around instead of permitting you to stay in the driver's seat. Maybe you were deeply hurt by someone you trusted, and now you are numb from the pain. Maybe you don't know why wonder is no longer present in your life, but life today is certainly lacking, as each day feels like the same predictable series of stressors and disappointments.

By now you may be thinking, "I thought this book was going to make me feel better about myself by helping me discover a creative life filled with magical things. So far it's filled with horrific stories of abuse and depressing insights into the ways I lie to myself."

This, my friends, is where the radical self-inquiry begins.

There is certainly no shortage of motivational self-help literature flooding the marketplace, filled with affirmations and truths about who you are, but the affirmations alone don't work from a neurological perspective. They certainly offer a story that is true, a story you're capable of living. But why doesn't the motivation stick? Why do we go from self-helping to self-sabotaging? Usually because we don't do the difficult work of examining the old story that conflicts with the new one being offered. It's like building a new house because the current one is falling down—but building that new house on a cracked foundation. It might be pretty at first, but before long, it's going to come crashing down again.

All stories have an inciting incident—a defining moment that changes things. Inciting incidents can lead to positive or negative change, like the moment in my story when I received a magic kit for Christmas, or the time I was abused a couple of years later. They become catalysts for change. After these moments, there is no going back to how things used to be.

Inciting incidents give birth to new chapters of our story. Let's consider the Transformation Map I introduced in chapter 1 with these inciting incidents in mind.

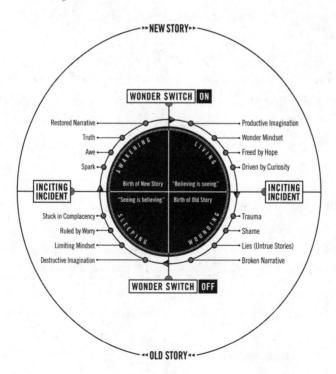

Notice that the birth of both an old story and a new story have the potential to directly follow these inciting incidents. If you follow the parts of my own story that I've shared so far, you can begin to see this cycle taking place. Like you, I came into this world wide awake to wonder, with the switch turned on. That meant I lived with hope and was driven by curiosity.

But what changed? I was broadsided by trauma. It led to shame that was rooted in lies, which gave birth to untrue stories. We take the stories we're told and the stories we experience—good or bad—along with the stories we tell ourselves and combine them all together to craft a narrative we consider to be the truth. The result for me was a broken narrative and the crushing of my wonder, followed by years lived in the bottom left quarter of the circle, stuck in a story I never would've chosen to write when my wonder switch was turned on.

Thankfully, the inciting incidents that surprise us are not always negative experiences. My capacity for wonder still existed, even when the switch was turned off. I came in contact with real magic, and it served as a spark, led to awe, opened me up to the truth, restored my narrative, and reawakened my wonder. That allowed me to spend years once again living in the top right quarter of the circle. And then, as you'll soon find out, everything came burning down again.

What narratives have you adopted as true? We need to reexamine those narratives and consider whether they are rooted in the truth. This process can be scary. You may have had a lot of high highs and low lows in your life. But when you participate in radical self-inquiry, reflection, and a path toward healing from trauma, it has the power to release you from the old story and change your life forever.

If you struggle to find and process your inciting incident, here are a few prompts that will help you discover the life-shaping moments in your story. Read each one and go with the one you feel most stirred and prompted by. The phrases may seem similar, but the subtle differences may help jog certain memories. It might help to pause your reading, grab a pen and a notebook or blank sheet of paper, and spend some time journaling your thoughts.

Tell me a story about a day when everything changed.

Tell me a story about an event that left you never the same.

Tell me a story about a time when you desperately wanted to give up.

Tell me a story about a season of your life you wish never would have happened.

Tell me a story about a moment when time seemed to stand still.

Inciting incidents are powerful, often shaping us far more than we realize. As you reexamine them, ask yourself, "What stories about who I am did this experience give birth to? And are those stories true? What are the actions I've taken as a result of the stories I made up about who I am?"

Once we adopt a narrative as true, even if it isn't, we seek information to support that narrative. We make choices that support that narrative. For example, let's say you tell yourself, "I'm a good parent." You'll seek out information and exhibit behavior that you are indeed your picture of what a good parent is. Likewise, if you tell yourself, "I'm a bad parent," you will work to interpret experiences through that filter of "I'm a bad parent," and your mind will lead you to make choices that support that story as truth. This same approach applies to general thought processes. You might say, "I am creative," and your brain works to confirm that that's true. What happens if you tell yourself the untrue story, "I'm not creative"? Yeah, you get the picture.

Clearly, not all stories we believe and tell ourselves are true. The next step, then, is to answer this simple yet powerful question: What stories are you telling yourself that *aren't* true? If you want to cultivate a life of wonder, with the opportunity to reimagine everything you thought was possible, you must do the difficult work of identifying the broken narrative you've adopted, the one driven by the lies that led you to deceive yourself. It's impossible to awaken your wonder if that broken narrative continues to lull your wonder back to sleep.

Revisiting the birthplace of your lies isn't fun, but there is good news: The truth, the lies—all of it is rooted in a story, and you are the storyteller. You can rewrite the story. That means you have the power to tear up the script that was handed to you and take some ownership in answering the question all stories try to answer: *What happens next?* And while you can't tear up the record of your past, you can retell those stories from a new perspective.

My experience with the girl in that high school gym led to the discovery of a matrix-like web of lies and deception. But with that discovery came another: the understanding that if deception is rooted in the stories we tell ourselves, then we also have the power to tell ourselves the truth.

It is through the unpacking of that untrue narrative that you are able to reclaim your childlikeness in a world that says, "Forget about the past and grow up. Stop being childish." But there's a huge difference between what is childish and what is childlike.

The story you hope for may be difficult to believe right now, simply because you can't see it. But seeing isn't believing—the belief system driven by your narrative is actually what determines what you see.

As a child, what did you see? Who were you before the world told you who you were supposed to be—before you were told or forced to grow up?

Believing Is Seeing

If I had a dollar for every time I heard someone say, "I'll believe that when I see it," I'd be a very wealthy man. One of my favorite ironies is how often I hear this in conversations that follow a magic show.

Night after night onstage, I perform illusions that lead people to see a variety of physical impossibilities:

A lady gets cut in half and put back together.

Objects levitate in midair, floating around as if by magic.

Thoughts that were once private are named out loud as minds are "psychically" read.

Personal possessions vanish into thin air, only to reappear in the strangest of places.

The list goes on and on.

None of these things are physically possible. I can't make anything levitate or read minds. Humans aren't psychic, and we have no supernatural powers. The tricks I perform onstage may look like magic, but they're just clever illusions. Why, then, do we call it magic? Because it sure looks like magic when performed flawlessly, doesn't it?

And that's the story that gets told as people exit the theater, even if they don't believe it to be literally true. "How was the show?" someone from the audience is asked. They reply, "It was amazing. I went up onstage and inspected everything. There were no strings.

No wires. No magnets. And then the table levitated right in front of my eyes. It was the craziest thing I've ever seen."

Seen.

Sure, they saw it with their own eyes. But was it real? Was seeing *really* believing?

Unfortunately, no. Seeing is not always believing, and we live in a world where things aren't always as they seem.

Multiple times now scientists have partnered with professional magicians to perform studies on the human brain to understand how our senses interpret information in the world around us and use it to form reality. Each time, studies confirm what we've always known: seeing is definitely not believing. But interestingly, what science also continues to show is that believing is actually seeing— that what we believe has the power to change what we see.

This is a valuable understanding in the context of the untrue stories we tell ourselves. But this isn't a new idea. Confirmation bias is something most of us studied in basic psychology in high school. What we believe tends to inform what we see, even if what we believe isn't true. We're in search of information to confirm those stories I keep bringing up—the ones we tell ourselves.

But what else might change about our lives by changing what we believe? If we expose the lies and believe the truth about who we are and are capable of being, is it also possible that we might be able to see things we couldn't see before? Is there magic—real magic—all around you, and maybe even inside you, that has been there all along? What if that magic hasn't been hiding? What if it has been in plain sight this whole time, and your belief systems have blinded you to it?

Have you ever had an experience where someone you know couldn't see the truth, even though it was right in front of them?

But everyone around them could see it and pondered, "Why can't they see it? It's right in front of their face."

Roald Dahl once wrote, "Those who don't believe in magic will never find it."[1] If you live as if seeing is believing, you'll be easily deceived and the lies will give birth to a cynical attitude that walks around thinking, "I'll believe it when I see it." And you'll never see the magic.

"But how do I believe?" I'm often asked.

Now that's a magical question. And like all magicians, I have a secret: wonder. Wonder is what gives you permission to believe in what you currently do not see.

You were meant for a life of magic. Not the counterfeit life you've been tricked into living by the stories you've been told and the stories you're telling yourself. A life that most people will never believe is possible, simply because they can't see it. A life many have tried to manifest or manufacture without ever challenging their status quo beliefs.

However, if you choose to believe—or perhaps more clearly, to allow your wonder to be reawakened so that you have the permission to believe—then you'll begin to see magic everywhere. Even in the mirror.

CHAPTER 4

Reawakening Wonder

Experience Real Magic Again

Ever heard the song "Your Body Is a Wonderland"? Those words aren't just a whimsical approach to a love song written by John Mayer. While I doubt he was musing on the biochemistry of the human body when he wrote them, it's science—your body is a wonderland.

One of my favorite discoveries of modern science is the connection between wonder and our physiology. Our wonder is connected to many facets of our physical health and overall wellness.

In my travels to deliver presentations at conferences and events, I am often faced with the challenge of introducing the subject of wonder to an audience in a short period of time. One of the initial challenges I sometimes face is a general apathy toward it, rooted in the assumption that it lacks relevance to our lives and the tasks at hand that seem to deserve far more immediate attention.

It's an apathy I can empathize with, but once you begin to understand the science behind wonder's impact on your body, it's hard not to lean in and want to know more. Naturally, the revealing of this research leads to a little more curiosity. One of the most common questions is "Where does wonder come from?"

I think we're naturally inclined to ask this question once we get a glimpse into what wonder has to offer us. If we can figure out where it comes from, maybe we can go to the source and grab a little for ourselves, like a magical pool we can dip our toes into and fill our cup with to take back home or to the office for when we need it. And if this magical pool doesn't exist somewhere, maybe we can just manufacture wonder whenever we need it.

In short, it's not that simple. But there are some things we can do. We can cultivate a life that increases the frequency of interactions with the golden pool of magic. And we can redeem our senses and awaken our awareness so when we touch that golden pool, we can absorb the fullest experience of wonder and all it has to offer us. And it has a lot to offer us. The more time we spend in that golden pool, the more our awareness changes, and therefore, the more magic we're able to regularly see and experience.

Wonder is the childlike state we find ourselves in when we are awake to possibility and rescued from the ordinary, granting us permission to believe in what we have yet to see. Wonder is often tied to awe. Though while wonder is inherently positive, awe may be either a positive or a negative experience. For this reason, awe is a possible pathway to wonder. For example, awe can be the emotional response when something negative surprises us and leaves us shocked and disappointed. Awe can also be the response to the real magic we experience in others, in ourselves, and in the world around us that leads us back to wonder. For this reason, awe and wonder aren't always good synonyms. You can be in awe but absent of wonder. After all, awe is the root of both the words awful and awesome.

I'm sure you've felt awe that left you speechless, as in "I can't believe he actually said that out loud" or "I can't believe she did that." Can you think of other examples? They may even have been moments that were awful but certainly didn't include an awakening of wonder.

This same line of thinking also applies when we witness a spectacle. Spectacles can leave us in awe or amazement, without our fully reaching a transformative experience of wonder. Perhaps that might be one way of thinking about wonder—its unique ability to leave us transformed. Spectacles are external events to which we are outside observers, while wonder is what happens when we allow ourselves to become *participants* in transformational stories. Transformation doesn't always happen overnight, though wonder is powerful enough that it can sometimes transform us in an instant. But something about wonder is transcendent and connected to transformation.

For example, I visited Disney World multiple times during my early twenties, a season in which my wonder switch was off. Those were years filled with apathy and cynicism as a result of a life entangled in lies. Surely "the most magical place on earth" could awaken my wonder, right? It most certainly could have, yet it didn't—though I had a blast each time I went.

One thing I made sure never to miss during my visits to any Disney park was the fireworks show at the end of the night. Whether surrounding the water at Epcot or gathered on Main Street in front of Cinderella's Castle at Magic Kingdom, we always saw quite a spectacle. Each time, I was amazed by Disney's ability to put on a show. Few others know how to put on a show like Disney. I experienced the spectacle, but I didn't experience wonder. What's the difference?

In my thirties, I was back at Disney World. Standing in front of that same castle at Magic Kingdom, I watched the same fireworks show fill the night sky that I had watched a decade earlier. But this time I had a four-year-old boy sitting on my shoulders. Jude marveled at the magic. For the first time as an adult, I experienced the spectacle of fireworks through the eyes of a child. I wasn't just being told a story by Disney; I found myself *in* the story they were telling, and it changed the story I was telling myself.

Magic tricks and fireworks make for a spectacular show, and if they lead people into an experience of wonder, the magic becomes real, even if the show still consists only of smoke and mirrors. It's not that some magicians perform tricks and others perform miracles—they're all tricks. We're "putting on a show." But a trick that tells a story and makes someone feel something and ask "what if?"—that's an experience, and it can be quite magical.

Another interesting observation connected to the research of awe is that the experience with my son was more communal than my previous visits to Disney. It wasn't that I had spent time in Disney parks alone, but they were with other people who at the time I did not share as close of a relationship with as I do with my son. New research hints that perhaps that's why it was more transformative and unforgettable to me. According to a study by UC Berkeley, when participants were in a positive state of awe, feelings of pride diminished. The wonder they felt contributed to feelings of smallness, not in the negative sense as one would often think in terms of smallness but in a way that brings about a reverence for the fact that we are but a small part of a greater whole, bringing about a sense of humility and a stronger sense of connectedness.[1]

Experiences that awaken our wonder don't make us want to zoom in; they make us want to zoom out and take it all in. For example, the Grand Canyon makes us want a vast, panoramic view; we want to step back to take more in. Experiences of awe that awaken our wonder help us shift our focus from ourselves to the connectedness of all things, including one another as human beings.

This reaction is because of what our brains do in positive awe-states to shift our physiology. Lab studies show a correlation between awe and a reduction in activation of the sympathetic nervous system. As the system that is associated with fight-or-flight responses, it works to regulate your body's unconscious actions. The more awakened you are to wonder, the more your sympathetic nervous system chills out, which means your heart chills out with it. Awe is calming. Instead of focusing on whether we should fight, flight, or freeze, we can simply be at peace, allowing us to reinvest our energy elsewhere, like the well-being of others.

This state of wonder can't be manufactured. It exists in response to magic that is already there. And awe stimuli (magic) are everywhere, all around us. Whether our wonder switch is on or off will determine the extent to which we experience the gifts offered by the feelings of awe that we experience..

Scientific researchers are just beginning to scratch the surface on the neurobiology of wonder. Neuroscience as a field of study itself is relatively new. The study of experiences and states like awe and wonder is even newer, so we are practically in our infancy of understanding. But we are beginning to understand. The human nature of connectedness, feelings, and embodiment and that human cells have aspirations—human cells have aligned to desire in the same way plants reach for the sun—are all connected to wonder.

New studies show that the human body is in its healthiest form when your mind (or your "soul") and body (which includes your brain) have regularly occurring experiences that leave you "filled with admiration, amazement, or awe."[2] It's as if we are hardwired to live with our wonder switches on, for when they're turned off, it isn't only the potential of our future stories that is affected but our physical health as well. It's as if wonder is like a nutrient, and we far too often suffer from a wonder deficiency.

I'm not exaggerating when I say that entire books have been written on the biological implications of wonder, and multiple clinical studies are now being conducted that show a clear connection between the state of wonder we find ourselves in and the response of our brains (not to be confused with our *minds*, though wonder certainly affects both).

Researchers' awareness of the connection between our minds and our bodies is not new. A study in 2002 by the Department of Psychiatry at the Ohio State University College of Medicine showed that negative emotions can intensify a variety of threats to the physical health of our bodies, including a range of diseases, often beginning with a degrading immune system and inflammation, which has been linked to cardiovascular disease, osteoporosis, arthritis, type 2 diabetes, Alzheimer's disease, even certain cancers, and more.[3] This link between the emotions we experience and the symptoms we physically feel in our bodies shows how both are interconnected.

The researchers go on to summarize their findings of the study by saying,

Production of pro-inflammatory cytokines that influence these and other conditions can be directly stimulated by negative emotions and stressful experiences. Additionally, negative emotions also contribute to prolonged infection and delayed wound healing, processes that fuel sustained pro-inflammatory cytokine production. Accordingly, we argue that distress-related immune dysregulation may be one core mechanism behind a large and diverse set of health risks associated with negative emotions. Resources such as close personal relationships that diminish negative emotions enhance health in part through their positive impact on immune and endocrine regulation.

If stress can have such a harmful impact on our health, is it possible that wonder could enhance our health? If feelings of isolation have such a negative effect on us physiologically, then could feelings of togetherness and connection boost our well-being? That's what researchers at UC Berkeley wanted to know. What they discovered may surprise you.

Perhaps following in the footsteps of previous studies showing the links between other positive emotions and physical health, a team of researchers at UC Berkeley set out to study the science of awe. Doing so led them to a treasure trove of findings. Our wonder impacts our entire lives. Wonder has the power to influence our physical health, our levels of empathy, the extent of our generosity with others, and even our sense of self. When we live in a state of wonder, we are not only healthier humans but better human beings.

A man recently came up to me after a keynote I had delivered on the power of the stories we tell ourselves. He was excited to tell me about a friend of his who had been volunteering her time to read stories to kids in children's hospitals and what a difference it was making. Perhaps there's a link between the way children's books awaken wonder and stir imagination in those kids and the way those experiences of wonder help their bodies heal.

Think about the ramifications of this.

We know our physical health is connected to our emotional health. So what if there are children lying in hospital beds right now as you read this book who could use wonder to give them a better chance at fighting off the illnesses plaguing their bodies?

If studies show that experiences of wonder are connected to an increase in empathy, would reawakening our wonder not change—or at the very least, slightly impact—the way we interact with those we disagree with? For example, what if the divisiveness of our current culture was connected to the loss of our wonder? Wonder could change how we treat each other. And not only in America. What might this mean for conflicts in regions of the world like the Middle East?

What if the brokenness of the criminal justice system in America could find restoration through an increase of empathy and a willingness to consider all the facts objectively? In one study, a subjective feeling of awe was so pleasant and calming that it permitted participants to pull attention away from themselves and refocus on the world around them, supporting the ability to take in more information and reduce their tendency to filter current experiences through what they thought they already knew. In short, experiences of wonder lead to a willingness to consider different narratives.[4]

In other words, wonder gives us permission to consider a new story and a willingness to consider that the current story we're telling ourselves may not be true after all. What if wonder could play a role in the mental health epidemic plaguing Americans? Even if it played only a small role, would it not be ludicrous to ignore the potential impact?

I know these are big questions, but maybe these things are possible. Because . . . science. What if?

Those same pro-inflammatory cytokines mentioned earlier that contributed to illness in response to negative emotion also respond to positive experiences of awe, making a strong case that wonder may decrease chronic inflammation in your body. Medical researchers have revealed that inflammation is one of the most powerful indicators of poor health and can shave as many as six to eight years off your life.

Emotional inflammation can also take place when your wonder switch is off. You end up burying your emotions, which can lead to your flaring up over the smallest thing at any given moment. The cycle of burying emotions and flaring up keeps you sick. When your wonder switch is off, emotional inflammation can lead you into all sorts of addictions and medicating behaviors, keeping you from flourishing.

Your body's cytokines are essential. They move cells to the appropriate area of your body to fight off things like disease and trauma. But if negative emotions and stressful experiences cause you to have high levels of cytokines, sustained over long periods of time, a variety of autoimmune diseases and even clinical depression can kick in.

In another study by UC Berkeley, researchers conducted two experiments where samples of gum and cheek tissue were taken and studied in correlation with the experience of positive emotions like awe, compassion, contentment, love, pride, and more. Results show that the experience of especially awe, wonder, and amazement had the lowest levels of the cytokine most closely linked with inflammation.[5] It's as if our bodies are wired for wonder.

But which came first, the chicken or the egg? Or in this case, do positive experiences of awe and the presence of wonder contribute to a decrease in inflammation in our bodies? Or does the absence of inflammation enable our wonder to be more easily awakened? The researchers of this particular study are on record saying they aren't yet sure. But there may be another clue that gives us the answer.

The Power of Suggestion

The mind is a powerful thing, and few things remind me of that truth more than the placebo effect.

The placebo effect is the idea that your mind can convince your body that a fake treatment—or no treatment at all—is real. Though commonly experienced in the form of a pill, like a sugar pill, for example, the placebo effect is experienced in a plethora of forms, ranging from acupuncture to homeopathic cures to the medical theater of hospitals. The lab coats, the stethoscopes, and the general theater of medicine, it turns out, increase your chances of being healed, simply through the way they contribute to the story your brain tells itself. Even seeing a nurse administer pain medication via your IV while you lie in a hospital bed is clinically shown to increase the effectiveness of the medication versus not personally witnessing the administration.[6]

Recent studies show that the placebo effect was 50 percent effective at fighting pain in response to a migraine attack.[7] Other studies show the placebo effect to be as high as 70 percent effective, often setting new standards for pharmaceutical companies in clinical trials.[8] Essentially, a drug is no longer considered effective unless it outperforms placebos, and with the effectiveness of these placebos, pharmaceutical companies have their work cut out for them.

Placebos impact more than just pain levels. They've been clinically proven to have profound healing powers in cases of anxiety and depression. In 2008 studies discovered that over a twelve-week period, placebo antidepressants were effective.[9] Another study showed an even more prevalent placebo effect in trials of anxiety medication.[10]

In the UK, a study at the School of Biosciences at Cardiff University showed a shocking placebo effect in cough medication trials.[11] *Medical News Today* states, "Eighty-five percent of the reduction in cough is related to treatment with placebo, and only 15 percent attributable to the active ingredient."[12] The mind is a powerful thing indeed.

More discoveries are being made on this subject every day. From many of the same autoimmune diseases mentioned previously to even erectile dysfunction in one study, the placebo effect continues to go beyond the confines of what many medical researchers ever thought possible. Perhaps the most valuable insight the placebo effect offers is in how it shows what happens when a belief becomes real—that our brain essentially heals itself by changing its expectations to meet reality, not vice versa.

This concept is hard to believe. But it's important enough and true enough that it bears repeating: our brain heals itself by changing its expectations to meet reality, not vice versa. I hope that alone motivates you to ensure that your stories are rooted in reality, not in lies and illusions.

The placebo effect is not alone in the ability to alter your supposed reality to match your expectations. Researchers are now studying the power of the nocebo effect, which is when patients knowingly participate in taking placebos and still experience healing effects. This phenomenon is echoed in the various examples of persuasion discussed in the previous chapter, such as confirmation bias or sensory deception, and in other powers of suggestion like hypnosis.

Hypnosis as a form of mind *control* has been debunked. The idea that hypnotists have a supernatural ability to put others into a trance and control their actions and behavior is simply not true. Around the world, however, there are countless reports of hypnotherapy in the form of *suggestion* helping people quit smoking, lose weight, conquer paralyzing phobias, and even become pregnant when they were formerly unable to.

One hypnotherapist in the UK commonly works with infertile women and shares verifiable reports of success. By working to change their belief systems surrounding the fears associated with being pregnant, she uses suggestion to "permit" their bodies to become pregnant. The obstacle beliefs are transformed, and then it's almost as if their intangible minds controlled the real and physical reproductive systems in their bodies. She says, "Every thought you think and every word you say forms a blueprint, and your mind must work to make that blueprint real."[13]

We are far more suggestible than we often realize.

Performing the art of illusion onstage for over twenty years certainly made me aware of how that suggestibility makes us susceptible to deception but also gives us access to the seemingly magical power to change our beliefs, and thereby change our realities.

Henry Ford once famously said, "Whether you believe you can do a thing or not, you're right."[14] That mindset contributed to his ability to accumulate a net worth of more than $200 billion dollars (adjusted for inflation), but it may also have helped him knock bad habits, cure his coughs, boost his mental health, and live to the age of eighty-three—twenty years longer than the average life expectancy of people born in the 1860s.

I am in no way an admirer of Ford's prejudice. His recorded anti-Semitism is deplorable. Again, your beliefs do not have to be true in order for them to be very real to you, but those beliefs drive your behavior. There are both very admirable and very despicable leaders who accomplish what they set out to achieve. They may not share the same character, but they share the common experience of believing in possibility instead of assuming failure.

To many people, especially those who have been taken captive by their cynicism, the words of Henry Ford and others like him are simply shrugged off as powerless positive thinking that has little to no impact on the lives we live from day to day. It's true that maybe Henry Ford lived to eighty-three because he went to the doctor when he got sick. That's what I do too, even though I believe in magic.

There is certainly an abundance of self-help information flooding the marketplace today, and much of it is rooted in nonsense. Not every sickness and disease can be healed with a sugar pill and a dose of happy thoughts. But a homeopathic remedy can remind us of the power of the placebo effect, and the supposed curse of a shaman can show us the power of suggestion. I am continually reminded that "believing is seeing" is far truer than "seeing is believing."

That's not feel-good woo-woo. It's feel-good science. And yet even though the research now exists, for many, the struggle to believe in anything that remains to be seen still feels impossible. If that's where you find yourself, I can relate. After all, I didn't wake up one day and choose to believe in magic again. Magic found me before I found it. That's how magic works sometimes.

Rediscovering the Magic

By the time I was thirty years old, I was "back on top." I'd dug out of debt, done some therapy, invested in my marriage, and traveled the world over. I'd done a portion of the "radical self-inquiry" I mentioned earlier. But that doesn't mean I was in a state of wonder, which is ironic, considering my work had taken me to over thirty countries on five continents. I'd visited plenty of the "wonders of the world."

I had stood at the edges of the Grand Canyon and Niagara Falls. I had walked the Great Wall of China. I had visited the Great Pyramids in Egypt multiple times.

The first time I saw the pyramids, I was in awe, but I looked at them the way most people look at a magician—less in awe and wonder and more in a manner of "I want to figure this out." I found the pyramids intriguing and perplexing, a mystery to be solved. My wonder had not yet been reawakened, and my apathy limited my experience at each of the world's wonders. I'd "been there and done that" and thought I had already experienced all the magic the world had to offer.

Perhaps the even greater irony is that what took me around the globe to experience the wonders of the world was my ability to make other people wonder, gifting them with experiences of awe and amazement. I just didn't realize that's what I was doing at the time. When you grow up studying the art of illusion from a young age, most of the focus is on the fooling. If magicians were to go on tour together, the back lounges of our tour buses would be filled with ramblings of "I really got 'em on that last one" or "They were completely fooled by that trick." The appeal, it seems, is in magic's ability to trick people—so much so that magic's greatest hit on TV at this time of writing is a show titled *Penn & Teller: Fool Us*.

When you perform magic tricks for a living, attempting to blur the line between illusion and reality, it's easy to lose your own point of reference for what is true. The most effective way to convince an audience that the illusion they're seeing is real is to believe it yourself. Of course, we know the tricks we perform *aren't* real, but to make a spectacle out of an illusion, we lose our grip on reality.

Night after night I was onstage, jumping into tanks of water wearing a straitjacket, or walking across shards of glass while barefoot, or taking a burning torch and putting it in my mouth to extinguish it, only to relight it as if by magic and then breathe a giant ball of fire into the air. Awe. Spectacle. Blurring the line between illusion and reality. Stunts and tricks. And then the night came when everything changed, when once again, the greatest trick was the one I played on myself.

I hosted a Fourth of July event, and I performed a fire-breathing act. I became arrogant. And I became foolish. I made a stupid mistake, and a stunt I had done successfully a few hundred times went horribly wrong.

After doing a few fire-eating stunts to warm up the crowd, like taking a lit torch and putting it into my mouth to extinguish it, I prepared to breathe a giant ball of fire. The last thing I remember was saying to myself, "I'm going to breathe the biggest, longest ball of fire the world has ever seen." Often pride really does come before the fall. As a giant ball of fire formed in front of me; the flames also managed to connect back to my lips. Naturally, the fuel in my mouth could no longer be contained behind my lips, and as it was released, it ran down my chin, setting part of my face on fire.

The flames burned for less than six seconds. I hadn't set myself up for success in case of emergency, but thankfully, the professional training I received that was being ignored up until that moment finally kicked in, and I calmly pulled off my shirt and placed it over my face. I was left with second-degree burns all over my face and mouth. I felt like the world's biggest idiot. And the pressure of putting on a show immediately took my mind to the pain that would soon head my way—not only the searing pain of the physical burns but also the ridicule of my peers.

By the time the night came to an end, I remember walking into our living room, lying down on the couch, looking at my wife, Kate, and saying, "It's pretty bad, isn't it?" It wasn't really an honest question. I knew it was bad. But she gave me a look of compassion that I can still recollect today and acknowledged that, yes, it was pretty bad. I slept on the couch that night to increase the chances of sleeping on my back without rolling over in the middle of the night. I remember struggling to fall asleep, my face feeling like it was still on fire, asking myself, "Why in the world do you do this stuff?"

Only a couple of short years earlier I'd almost not held my breath for the full four minutes that it usually took me to escape from a straitjacket and tank of water while performing Houdini's famous Water Torture Cell Escape. A couple of years before that, I'd had a near miss performing an escape appropriately called the Table of Death. My entire crew stood sidestage in the wings, screaming at me in the middle of the performance because at any moment a giant rack of five hundred pounds of steel bars and spikes was about to fall and crush one of my legs.

Sure, I'd had some close calls. But every professional who performs frequently and at a high level has made mistakes and had some close calls. If you play with fire, as they say, you're eventually going to get burned, especially if you get arrogant and foolishly break the safety rules you were taught to always follow. But after the fire-breathing accident, something was different. I was ready to quit.

There were others who were ready for me to quit too. In a Facebook group for performers, there was a thread about my accident. It was filled with a slew of hateful comments making fun of my mistake. One commenter even said, and I quote, "Too bad he didn't die." I was later told it was because this person didn't like my worldview and presentation style. Being ridiculed by your peers never feels good, but a portion of what they said was accurate. I had made a pretty obvious mistake, and I knew better. As for the rest? Well, I'd been there before—the words of bullies were nothing new.

"Harris, why do you do this stuff?" many friends asked.

I continued to ask myself that same question in the days and weeks of healing that followed.

At the time, I had forgotten. I had forgotten the look of awe on my mom's and dad's faces when I put that little red ball inside that vase and made it disappear twenty-one years earlier. I had forgotten the way their reactions reawakened the wonder that the bullies on my playground had crushed. I had forgotten why I did magic. And when I lost my why, I lost my way. I had lost my wonder, and my belief in magic went along with it.

About the time I was ready to hang up my proverbial top hat and quit, I finally stopped staring at the ceiling and started looking down at my living room floor, and it was as if a bright spotlight shone down from high above. What it lit up on that living room floor changed everything.

Nine months earlier my wife had given birth to our first child—our son, Jude. The experience of watching a child be brought into this world will chip away at the tough exterior surrounding the hardest of hearts, as it had begun to chip away at mine. Over the course of those nine months, I'd spent time with Jude. I'd held him in my arms and played with him. But this time, the experience of interacting with him was different.

I saw his baby blue eyes look around, seeing the magic in seemingly every little thing. With my workaholism halted against my will, the forced pause of my injury brought with it a lot more watching and listening and a lot less performing and talking. I had seen my son. I had already begun working to slow down and really *see* him, but I had yet to see the world through his eyes. Once I did, it was as if the scales fell from mine.

Jude saw real magic everywhere. I remember lying on the couch, feeling the pain as my cracked, burned lips stretched into a smile as Jude giggled at the simplest of things. I remember the look of awe in his eyes as a prism of color dashed across the ceiling from the light that refracted through our front window each time a car drove down our street in the afternoon sun. I remember his look of determination each time he fell down while trying to get up and walk, because despite failing over and over again, it was as if, in his mind, anything was possible.

As Jude got older and my face got better, we'd go out and do things I used to take for granted, like blowing the seeds off dandelions while running through our backyard or dashing through the dark, catching fireflies in jars. I remember blowing bubbles and seeing just bubbles but looking at Jude's eyes and realizing he was seeing magic. They weren't just bubbles. To a little kid whose wonder is wide awake, there's no "just" anything. Only magic.

I began to believe in real magic again. And it occurred to me how ironic it is that people call us "magicians," when all we do is clever illusions. Everything you see a magician do onstage is fake. And yet we look at the magic in the world around us, roll our eyes in cynicism, and shrug it all off as fake.

Before my cynicism crushed my kids' wonder, my kids flipped the switch and reawakened wonder in me, and I began to see the magic again. With that renewed ability to see the magic, I rediscovered my "why," and the way forward became clear. I was no longer interested in performing tricks to show the world what is fake; I was committed to performing those tricks to remind others of what is real.

Maybe you've been doing what you do for so long that you've forgotten why you fell in love with it in the first place. Whatever it is, you caught a glimpse of magic and it beckoned you. Maybe it's not your vocation—maybe it's a hobby or a dream you've shelved for years because somewhere along the way your wonder was crushed, and the magic, and the purpose that went along with it, was lost.

If you want to find clues that lead you to turn your wonder switch back on, it helps to understand that your "why" is a source of wonder. If you're going through the motions without a why—a purpose—wonder won't thrive in that environment.

Your why is something you once saw magic in, or something that helped you realize the magic in you. The magic you witnessed and experienced captivated you, stirred your imagination, and drew you in. You were driven to be part of that magic. My friend Brad Montague calls it your "wonder work."

When we're doing our wonder work in the world, we thrive. It often leads to what many would consider success. But when success equates to a focus on the what, you begin to lose your why. And when you lose your why, you lose your way.[15]

The magic Jude saw while crawling around on our living room floor was there for me to see all along. But I couldn't see it, partially because I didn't believe in it. Wonder wasn't there to give me permission to believe in what I had yet to see. I'm not alone. Often many of us are physically awake but far from being fully aware.

Living a creative life filled with magic starts with the art of "waking up." Turning on the wonder switch is the equivalent of waking up. It brings about an openness—an openness to the reality that maybe there really is more going on around you than you previously realized. An openness that maybe there's more to your story.

Real magic is the extraordinary that exists all around us in the seemingly ordinary, often right in front of our eyes. It can't be manufactured. It already exists, and there is no magic wand that gives you the power to control or summon it. It is real. It is in you and all around you. The goal, then, is to be able to see and experience it. To fully experience it requires two things.

The first requirement is belief. It is the belief in magic that gives you the ability to see it. And remember, wonder is what gives you permission to believe.

The second is an openness to magic so that you are able to experience what it has to offer and say to you. And maybe more than an openness, an awareness. Magical experiences are transcendent and transformative, and they occur all the time, but we miss them because, though we aren't physically asleep, it's as if our eyes are closed. In his book *Soulful Spirituality*, Dr. David Benner writes,

"Living with awareness is a prerequisite to becoming deeply human."[16] I don't think you have to consider yourself "spiritual" to agree.

Remember, wonder is our natural state. We were born wide awake to wonder, which means we don't have to go find something we don't have the capacity to attain—rather, we have to turn back toward what was always there. Our wonder switches have simply been turned off and are waiting to be turned back on.

If you don't wake up, the world will pick your pockets clean. But it won't just steal your wallet; it will empty your wallet and put it back in your pocket stuffed full of counterfeit bills. If you aren't tuned in and paying attention, those counterfeits will trick you into thinking you never missed a thing. The difference between a petty thief who steals your wallet and has to run and a professional pickpocket who never gets caught is that the professional steals your wallet and replaces it with something of equal weight and size. Your brain doesn't realize your wallet is gone because it feels a counterfeit it believes to be real.

It's kind of like that scene in *Indiana Jones* where Indy tries to steal an ancient artifact and attempts to rapidly replace the artifact with a little bag of sand. The artifact and the bag of sand aren't equal. If the fake felt equal to what was once there, nothing or no one would ever notice, and Indy would walk right out without a hitch. If his sleight of hand were a little smoother, he would have made for a good thief.

Counterfeits are dangerously powerful because they desensitize us. Because they *feel* real, we go on living, thinking that what we have *is* real. Your life is filled with magic you don't call magic. But real magic has always been there. And it's time to wake up to it.

When you awaken your wonder, you don't simply find yourself

in a state of rest for the remainder of your life. Wonder changes things. Ultimately, wonder leads to action. Wonder can be a powerful impetus, and can even shape our identity, because our experiences of wonder help tell us who we are. Let's continue to explore who we are, together, by examining one of the most powerful forces that makes you uniquely human—your imagination—and how the position of your wonder switch determines how you put it to work.

CHAPTER 5

A New Story

*Changing the Way You Use
Your Imagination*

What is your greatest fear? What does it look like? What does it sound like? What does it feel like? Have something in mind? Now think about it for a moment. Really, take a moment to bring it to mind. Where does your mind take you?

If you stop to think about your greatest fear, the experience is likely less about naming and more about storytelling. Did you blurt out a fear while reading, like spiders or heights or being alone forever? More likely, you conjured up an image in your imagination, the way a set designer brings to life the scene of a film.

Your imagination has been referred to for ages as your "mind's eye." But if seeing isn't always believing, is it also possible that what your mind's eye sees is not always what you get? As Mark Twain once said, "You can't depend on your eyes when your imagination is out of focus."[1] And that was way back in 1889, before neuro-scientists confirmed that believing is seeing.

In 2016 I had begun to shift my work from traveling the world telling stories on stages and screens all by myself to a vision that included other people who shared a belief in the power of stories. Those changes eventually led to my leading a community of story-tellers referred to simply as "STORY." What started as a two-day conference in Nashville has blossomed into a global community of thousands of writers, filmmakers, photographers, performing artists, marketers, communicators, designers, and a variety of other storytellers.

The STORY community still gathers both physically and vir-tually for a two-day conference-style event each year for creative inspiration and meaningful conversations around the powerful role storytellers play in the world. We now have participants from all walks of life, including freelancers just beginning their careers as creative professionals to veteran storytellers from companies like Apple, Google, Disney, and many more.

Leading this community has taught me so much and has played a huge role in ensuring that the wonder my kids awakened in me stays fully alive and well. That should come as no surprise because STORY is a community made up of some of the most cre-ative people in the world.

One thing that surprised me about this community, how-ever, was the common thread of fears and insecurities associated with living a creative life. Regardless of the level of success many achieve, they struggle with a stream of constant worries, ranging from rejection to imposter syndrome.[2] My team and I partnered with behavioral storytelling specialist David Paull, along with his amazing staff of researchers. David is the CEO of Dialsmith and

Engagious. Their work often focuses on the intersection of story-telling and behavioral science.

We began with a ten-minute survey of 108 STORY conference attendees prior to the conference. Each participant ranked twenty-two fears based on the impact each fear has on his or her life. Here are the top five fears that prevent them from being successful:

1. not living up to expectations
2. being judged negatively
3. being rejected
4. making a bad decision
5. disapproval from others

All these fears are anchored in the perceptions and judgments of others. They also happen to be rooted in shame and can be traced back to experiences before the age of ten.

These fears take our imagination hostage and absorb our creative energy. We all want to be connected to others. We want to fit in and be accepted. These necessities are hardwired into our very survival. Your central nervous system sees "belonging" as "life," and "not belonging" as "death." No wonder these things lead to "the show" we spend our lives performing.

As we noticed these common worry threads, we desired to curate live experiences that would help people overcome these worries. This process continually led me back to research around the human imagination. Do our minds do what they want to do or what we tell them to do? What is "imagination"? What power does it hold?

The imagination has been a mystery to us for millennia and, in many ways, remains mysterious still today to modern psychologists and neuroscientists alike. Some of what we do know is that even though imagination is often studied in conjunction with creativity, creative thinking is more complex than we've often been led to believe. It is a common myth that creative thinking happens only on one side of our brain, while the other side, the left brain, is used merely for tasks that have to do with logic, like science and mathematics. But this isn't the case. Your imagination does not exist in your right brain alone.

The part of your brain that is called on when you imagine situations based on personal experiences is now known as the brain's "default network," essentially your imagination circuit.[3] It's the "moviemaking" part of your brain that imagines or reimagines something from your past and comes up with potential scenarios for your present and future. Interestingly, this default network is found equally in both the left brain and the right brain. Labeling a coworker by saying, "Well, he's just more right brain than left brain," or vice versa, as a way of excusing what is commonly misunderstood to be a lack of imagination just doesn't hold up.

This is why when we read or hear famous quotes about imagination from the geniuses who came before us, like Albert Einstein, we shouldn't allow our cynicism to write them off as simply feelgood positive thinking. Einstein once said in a 1929 interview, "Imagination is more important than knowledge. Knowledge is limited. Imagination encircles the world."[4] We should take these statements for what they are: science. Our bodies are wired to imagine, and there are physical, tangible parts of our brain that support this tool we've been given to see and then create the future.

"Logic," Einstein added, "will get you from A to B. Imagination will take you everywhere."[5]

Reminding ourselves of the significance of imagination is

important because everything in the world works so hard to crush our wonder, destroying our imagination along with it. Wonder gives us permission to believe more is possible, while our imagination is the tool we use to visualize images of these possibilities.

The cynicism that is so rampant in our world certainly pushes back against the notion that imagination is more important than knowledge, doesn't it? It doesn't take a very long look at America's education system to come to the understanding that information and our ability to absorb it are of the utmost priority. This leaves us to think, "Sure, Einstein, imagination sounds nice. But if you want to truly succeed in today's world, the secret is to study hard in school."

This was certainly my experience of childhood education, and even most of my undergraduate studies at a liberal arts college. In his popular TED Talks and other online videos, Sir Ken Robinson shares the importance of imagination.

> We have this extraordinary human power, the power of imagination. We take it totally for granted.
>
> This capacity to bring to mind things that aren't present, and on that basis to hypothesize about things that have never been but could be. Every feature of human culture in my view is the consequence of this unique capacity. Now other creatures may have something like it. Other creatures sing, but they don't write operas. Other creatures are agile, but they don't form Olympic committees. They communicate, but they don't have festivals or theater. They have structures, but they don't build buildings and furnish them. We are unique in this capacity.[6]

Sir Robinson continues, "The capacity that produced the most extraordinary diversity of human culture, of enterprise, of innovation, six thousand languages currently spoken on earth, but I believe we systematically destroy this capacity in our children and in ourselves."[7]

He's right. We take one of the most powerful resources for human flourishing and crush its potential by destroying its capacity. But that doesn't mean our imaginations aren't active.

The Misuse of Imagination

When wonder is awake, we use our imagination the way we did as children—to dream, create, innovate, and solve problems. We immersed ourselves in stories of make-believe that were filled with possibility. When wonder dies, our ability to innovate in productive ways dies with it. But because our imagination is always active and creating or filling in the blanks of a story, we use it to worry.

It takes the same amount of energy and effort to create a positive vision as it does to create a negative one. In fact, because worry is so bad for your health, it may even take more energy to create a negative one.

Worry is a misuse of our imagination.

When you worry, you make assumptions about things in the future that often do not happen. For example, say you just got a new job and therefore a new boss. It's your first week at work, and you're worried about how your boss will respond to a project you've been asked to work on. When you worry while you work, you're not only drained of energy and less productive but also feel rushed, which leads to stress, which leads to not producing your best work. You might even feel sick. Your body will do everything in its power to avoid a bad ending to the story your mind is imagining.

Or take your finances, for example. Ever worry about those? I know I have. Worrying about money leads to stress, making it hard to sleep. Worry can make you irritable and cause problems in your relationships, creating drama. We'll discuss that drama more in a few moments because your imagination loves drama the way your taste buds love sugar. (It's almost as if my taste buds exist for consuming ice cream.) If you don't have a worthy and engaging problem to solve, your imagination gets bored. Then instead of using it to come up with a solution—a positive vision for the future—you keep devoting your time, energy, and attention to worry.

Worry is a trap. When you are caught up in it, it becomes a straitjacket constraining your life, and the only way out is to flip on the wonder switch and use your imagination to create a positive vision of the future. If you don't, the hope of escape doesn't exist, and you'll settle for a life riddled with the pain and suffering of worry and anxiety.

When I lead workshops with corporate teams, I often bump into self-limiting mindsets around the subject of imagination and creativity. "I'm not creative," I often hear. Or, "We're not the creatives," as if creativity were reserved only for those worthy of being adorned with the title. I cringe at how often I hear the use of the word *creative* as a noun. No one is *a creative*. Everyone is creative. It is possible to practice being more creative, and some people are creative professionals because creativity is their focus and vocation. Sure, it's semantics, but words matter.

My friend Marc Pimsler, who is a leading expert in the field of experiential therapy and so much more, once explained to me that access to creativity and spontaneity are two primary barometers of mental health. In his words, "It's not if you have it but whether or not you access it."

Reserving the word *creative* for certain teams or departments within our organizations—or even a select few of our friends—shifts our mindsets and restricts our ability to unleash our imaginations to create and dream the way we're truly capable of. If you're a professional designer or copywriter or advertising guru at a creative agency and are obsessed with calling yourself a "creative," please stop. Each time we label a certain team or group as "the creatives" or person as "a creative," we imply to others that they *aren't* creative. Not everyone is an artist, but every human being is highly creative, and we all have the potential to channel that creativity into any hobby, outlet, or vocation of our choosing.

If you sense any passion here, it's because I come in contact with this belief on a regular basis. I recently had a conversation with an event attendee who simply said, "I'm just not creative like everyone else is at this conference." I asked a series of follow-up questions in an effort to understand how this person used his imagination. It turns out he wrote Oscar-worthy screenplays in his head, and he was in the starring role. He, as the main character, was in all types of imaginative situations. His story just lacked the right ending. It was one of the most dramatic stories I'd ever heard, filled with a treacherous journey navigating an abundance of challenges, fears, and anxieties—the stuff great stories are made of. But in the version of the story he was imagining, he wasn't transformed by the journey and didn't end up in a more beautiful place. His creative energy was certainly being spent; it was just being misused.

So many of us have experienced wounding in the midst of a creative act, so we learned to shut it down to avoid being hurt again.

Think about how much time we spend each day imagining all the horrible things that could possibly go wrong, even though we have no real evidence or sign that those things would ever happen. Sure, we fear that they may happen, but those fears are rarely rooted in any sort of proof that they might come to fruition. It's not that this person wasn't using his imagination. His imagination was surprisingly active. But his imagination was being misused, likely in an attempt to self-protect from the repeat of a previous wound. He needed healing from that wound and a healthier perspective, shifting his mindset from worry to possibility. He needed his wonder switch turned on to permit him to believe in what he couldn't yet see.

This is why on the Transformation Map, we find both "productive imagination" and "destructive imagination."

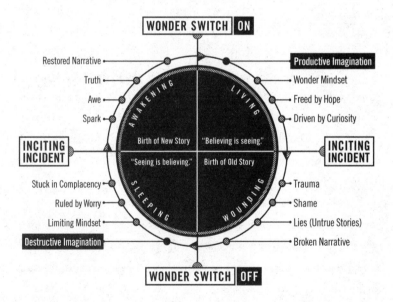

As you can see, imagination is a part of the full circle, no matter what part of the story you find yourself in. But where you are in your journey, and whether your wonder switch is on or off, determines not *if* you put your imagination to work but *how* you put your imagination to work.

Rational Fear versus Irrational Fear

To be clear, not all fear is bad. If you were never scared, you'd probably be dead by now. Instead, you're reading or listening to this book about reimagining your future. What's the difference between rational fear and irrational fear?

The shortest answer is that rational fear keeps us alive—survival instincts are there for a reason. Irrational fear is killing us—literally. As noted in the previous chapter, negative emotions and stressful experiences cause a variety of autoimmune diseases and even depression. Try to cut yourself some slack, because fear is a natural human emotion. We all experience fear throughout the course of our lives. What matters is whether you control your fears or your fears control you.

Your body is programmed to feel fear. Your nervous system, as also discussed previously, triggers your survival instincts and causes you either to freeze, to put up a fight, or to run away as quickly as possible. These instincts helped you survive childhood and continue to serve you in adulthood through a heightened sense of awareness of potential risks or threats. Maybe you instinctually got a bad vibe from a stranger and immediately sought the safety of a parent or loved one. Or maybe you experienced a red flag on a date or at a job interview because something "felt off." If so, that was the modern equivalent of your nervous system saying, "Run from the lion if you want to live."

This kind of fear can be healthy because it serves a purpose: keeping us safe. Though fear is typically classified as a feeling, this kind of fear has less to do with your mind and more to do with the biology of your brain, making it far more rational. If you're riding in a car while a friend is driving recklessly, for example, and you experience physical symptoms like an accelerated heart rate, higher blood pressure, and sweaty palms, that's your body's way of saying, "Change the situation. I don't feel safe right now." And for good reason. Your creative imagination is telling you a story, and your body doesn't want the fictional story in your head to become a reality. Speak up and honor that fear, because it's trying to keep you alive.

What about unhealthy fear? The irrational kind that is likely often stimulated by wounding and shame messages that lead us to see danger that is merely perceived but not actually dangerous? Where does the "dark side" of your imagination take you?[8]

You've probably heard the age-old acronym for FEAR—false evidence appearing real. Sure, it sounds cheesy, but there's probably a reason it became so commonplace. When it comes to irrational fears, it's a pretty accurate and useful acronym. Sometimes even though the evidence triggering our worry may not be rooted in reality, it is informed by the trauma and experiences of our past, often related to our relationships with others.

Time and again we're forced to retrace and connect the dots between the stories we've been told and the stories we're telling ourselves. And often the stories we've been told by others came without words because they came in the form of actions and abuse instead. What ghosts still follow you? What continues to whisper lies, feeding the dark side of your imagination?

All Problems Are "People Problems"

The Christmas of my freshman year of high school, my uncle gave me cash. I spent every penny of it on a T-shirt from Abercrombie & Fitch. Abercrombie was the "it" brand in my small town in 1999.

At the time, half my wardrobe came from yard sales or was hand-me-downs, so buying that shirt made me feel like a rich kid.

I don't know what made me think it was a good idea at the time, or why it never occurred to me that others would notice, but I wore that shirt to school at least twice a week. The T-shirt was basic white with navy blue letters spelling out the name of the brand. I'll never forget that shirt. I'll never forget it because, like many things I attempted to find my identity in, it was a sign of my insecurity, rooted in the fear of not fitting in.

In her bestselling book *Daring Greatly*, Brené Brown says we can find belonging only when we are willing to accept ourselves. She writes, "Because true belonging only happens when we present our authentic, imperfect selves to the world, our sense of belonging can never be greater than our level of self-acceptance." Presenting our authentic selves requires bravery. Brown later writes, "Courage starts with showing up and letting ourselves be seen."[9]

Why does allowing ourselves to be seen for who we really are require such courage? Perhaps it's because we don't like who we are, and heaven forbid we allow others to see us the way we see ourselves in the mirror. Where does this fear come from?

In the twentieth century, two names rose to fame in the world of psychology. Austrian neurologist Sigmund Freud and Swiss psychiatrist Carl Jung are psychoanalysts you have probably heard of before, and maybe you even studied them in school. But there was a third thought leader from the same era, also from Austria, whose views and theories remained lesser known but have recently found their way into more of our modern dialogue and understanding of psychology. His name is Alfred Adler.

Both Adler and Freud were medical doctors who were among the first to use the new field of psychology to help their patients improve their physical health, yet they ended up disagreeing over some fundamental differences in how the trauma of our past has a cause-and-effect relationship with our present and future.

Adler introduced a theory called "individual psychology." I was first introduced to Adler in a thought-provoking book titled *The Courage to Be Disliked*.[10] The book is written as a dialogue between two characters, a philosopher and a student. It turns out Adler's theories are as philosophical as they are psychological.

One of the most interesting of Adler's views was his belief that all problems are interpersonal relationship problems. It might feel a little far-fetched to say that all problems are basically "people problems," but as you have read through so much of my own story, my life certainly confirms this to be true.

The bullies on the playground in elementary school. Burying my deepest, darkest secrets despite the burden of my untold story. Wasting a million dollars to try to trick others into liking me. Wearing a T-shirt with blue letters on it two days a week. All these problems were driven by interpersonal relationship problems.

Driven by the innate desire to experience love and belonging, we do everything in our power to earn the approval of others, leading our imaginations to spend far too much effort creating false narratives around what might happen if that approval never comes.

What if, instead, you started down the path of healing from the pain of what wounded your wonder? From a restored place of wonder, you could reinvest all the creative energy being spent worrying—imagining the ways you're going to fail or be rejected— into reimagining what might be possible instead. Though complete control of every facet of your life is ultimately an illusion, you have far more control over yourself than you do over the reactions and responses of others. You can't control what people think about you any more than I can control what people think about me. And I'm a professional when it comes to tricking (i.e., persuading) people.

Once I realized I had no control over whether someone would love and accept me or take advantage of me, I developed the courage to be disliked. Instead of constantly worrying what other people thought, I wondered what my life could be like if I made peace with who I was. Making peace with who I was helped me find the courage to allow myself to present my authentic, true self to others, willing to be seen as the strange, quirky weirdo I am.

I should point out that Adler never taught that just because you can stop attempting to control the opinions of others through the pursuit of self-acceptance doesn't mean interpersonal relationships don't matter. He strongly believed in the practice of placing confidence in others through horizontal relationships rather than vertical ones. Horizontal relationships are relationships in which everyone is treated as equals. Vertical relationships are hierarchical and aren't as naturally committed to the contributions of others. I'd encourage you to do more research on Adler's theories. Though his ideas and writings are more than a century old, they feel incredibly timely. But Adler's view of etiology versus teleology is most relevant to the subject of this book.

Etiology is the science of finding causes and origins. Teleology is more of a statement of something's purpose. Etiology would ask what triggered the writing of this book. What was the cause that triggered the effect? A teleological view would ask what my desired outcome was and would explore how that desire motivated the action of writing.

Adler's falling-out with Freud was in response to Freud's etiological philosophy. Freud believed etiological causes drive human behavior. His theories have shaped much of the trauma theory put into practice by therapists today. It makes sense that when we are confronted with an overwhelming traumatic experience, regardless of our age, that experience is integrated into the narrative of our life. This creates a logical cause and effect in the stories we tell ourselves.

In a book that has become legendary, especially among storytellers, *The Power of Myth* author Joseph Campbell writes, "Freud tells us to blame our parents for all the shortcomings of our life, and Marx tells us to blame the upper class of our society. But the only one to blame is oneself."[11]

Adler would have liked Joseph Campbell. Adler too believed this sort of cause-and-effect trauma theory to be misunderstood. He instead focused on the misguided teleological roots of our neurosis, which led to an exploration of what we want and whether our current choices are helping us attain our desires. He didn't believe that our behavior is driven primarily by the trauma of our past but rather that we act and feel a certain way because we choose to—and conveniently exploit the circumstances of our past to justify our actions. In other words, we use our imagination to create whatever narrative we're willing to live with to like ourselves.

This dismissal of the impact of trauma feels shortsighted in light of what we now understand today. My draw to Adler's focus on the "here and now" is found in the fact that it so often feels missing from the conversation by so many. However, there is no doubt that power is contained in not only the here and now but also the "there and then." Leading mental and emotional health professionals see benefit in both because both the past and the present need our attention.

Let me give you a simple example. There was a time this past summer when my schedule was getting the best of me. I had a creative brief due to one of the clients of our consulting practice for a live experience my company was designing and producing for them, and the deadline approached far more quickly than I had anticipated. Like cranking out a paper in school the night before it's due, I waited far too long to build the pitch deck I needed to build for the presentation. It wasn't because I didn't have the time—I just used my calendar as an excuse. One of our team members expressed some frustration to me that she wasn't able to prepare for our client meeting the way she had hoped and felt she was going into our pitch blind.

Often in a scenario in which we receive a negative response to our work—whether from a family member or a client or in this case a member of my team—most of us are indignant, swearing up and down that we did our best work and gave it everything we could. That's exactly what I did, which could only mean that the reason for the resulting conflict with my team was that this person didn't like me or, at the least, didn't understand me. In our minds, we genuinely believe we made our best effort; the other person must not have understood how much effort we gave.

After all, you crunched when the time came and stayed up until the wee hours of the morning to finish important work. The caveat is that if we were to think long and hard about how this could have happened, we would see that we didn't prioritize our time and attention appropriately, ultimately not giving the project the attention it deserved, which resulted in conflict or less than desirable feedback.

Why do we go through this overly complicated thought process? Because we're desperate for love and belonging. And for some of us, when we don't feel we have it, our imagination can't help itself in following its creative process of dreaming up all sorts of interpersonal relationship nightmares. Before we know it, our lives are ruled by worry instead of wonder. What does it look like to choose wonder over worry instead?

Have you accepted yourself as you truly are? Trust me, I know from personal experience that it's far easier said than done. It's something I struggle with still today. But it's a necessary step back toward wonder, and when you take that step, you begin to realize that the act of love toward yourself and others becomes one of fear's and worry's greatest antidotes. Love equals belonging. Love leaves little room for fear. Love lifts us up where we belong.[12]

The more open you are to love, in all its various forms—from divine, unconditional love, to romantic love in an intimate relationship, to the love of family and friends—the more love you allow into your life, the more your wonder will reawaken and the more your worries will fade, all the while permitting your imagination to create and dream in ways you never thought possible.

Look for Better Drama

Are you using your imagination to dream and create rather than to worry and be consumed by all the drama that comes from interpersonal relationships? If so, maybe the path to less worry and drama is as simple as keeping your imagination busy by focusing on other problems that you have more control over.

When your imagination gets bored, it looks for something to feed on. The human brain was created to solve problems. And if you don't have a high-level problem worthy of solving, the brain will create one, usually in the form of drama. Steven Pressfield says, "Creating soap opera in our lives is a symptom of Resistance.

Why put in years of work designing a new software interface when you can get just as much attention bringing home a boyfriend with a prison record?"[13]

Have you ever caught yourself doing this?

Maybe you're carrying too much stress at work, and little things that usually wouldn't be a big deal turn into major drama at home. When a partner leaves a mess in the kitchen, it is such a personal offense it triggers a fight. Or a family member gets an earful because they "just don't understand," and you're tired of telling them something "a million times." Was it really a million times? Or how about that time you saw a post on Instagram with a photo of a group of friends, only you weren't in it? Did you attempt to mind-read and project ulterior motives? What kind of dramatic storytelling did that kick-start in your head?

Imagine if you could free yourself from all the internal drama you drum up. Imagine what you could do with all that energy instead. What would it look like to engage in better drama? What if you turned your "people problems," and even the trauma others caused, into creativity? What role does the trauma in your past play in your capacity to upcycle it as creative fuel that feeds your imagination in positive ways? Quite a bit, according to what feels like endless piles of research.

Let's look at some examples of how we can use trauma to fuel our creativity. An organization called the American Art Therapy Association regularly publishes its findings in *Art Therapy*, often showcasing the effectiveness of art therapy and creative writing as a way of healing from the pain of our past.

Another example is Allison Fallon, who has helped hundreds of authors fulfill their dream of writing a book (including the one you're reading or listening to right now), and who has helped countless others to write simply as a way of healing from trauma, with astonishing results.[14]

CreatiVets, a nonprofit based in Nashville, helps soldiers who have come home from war with PTSD successfully find healing through art and music. Using various forms of art, including songwriting, CreatiVets pairs veterans with songwriters and music artists to allow them the opportunity to express their story through song. Doing so helps veterans begin to heal from service-related trauma by fostering self-expression in a way that "allows them to transform their stories of trauma and struggle into an art form that can inspire and motivate continued healing."[15] Their programs are showing incredibly high rates of success and progress. How amazing is that?

Bethany Haley Williams is doing similar work with former child soldiers in Africa. As the founder and executive director of Exile International, she is leading the way in helping children traumatized not only by war but also by being forced to fight as soldiers in them. With a PhD in counseling psychology, a license in clinical social work, and twenty years of experience working with emotionally wounded children, Bethany has found the greatest success in rehabilitating war-affected children through—you guessed it—art.

Similar to the way a storyboard artist would map out a Hollywood film, Bethany and her team lead children through the process of expressing the pain and brokenness of their stories through pictures. She also teaches them to dream again and to refocus their imaginations on a hope-filled future. Doing so assists with finding redemption amid horrific suffering, in ways similar to how a character in a film ends up being shaped by the conflict of their journey.

Uneducated, third-world children who have been forced to spend years of their childhood fighting in war fields instead of learning in classrooms may not know how to write out their stories, but they understand the universal language of pictures. How much more power is there in putting down a rifle and picking up a crayon? As Bethany is teaching us, more than we often realize.

The reason these forms of experiential therapy are so effective is because creative acts stimulate the lower right hemisphere, the limbic system. This also happens to be the part of the brain where trauma is stored. Trauma is a full-body experience. Experiential therapy is effective because it takes the experience of trauma and replaces it with a healing experience, not much different from moving from an old story to a new one.

Marc Pimsler, a friend I mentioned earlier, now helps lead the International Society for Experiential Professionals. Their organization is leading the way in this highly effective form of experiential therapy and doing groundbreaking work in helping us find the healing we so desperately need in order to find our way back to wonder.

These views have been echoed by countless artists who have turned to their pain throughout their creative processes, like painter Paul Klee when he said, "I create—in order not to cry."[16] These kinds of sentiments often trigger an eye roll and lead the cynical voice that has been ingrained in us to say, "Oh, please. Sure, go paint away your sorrows. I'll drink away mine." But once again, the research backs up what many imaginative artists have felt all along—that engaging our imaginations in acts of creation can, in fact, help us heal from the experiences that brought us tears and, in turn, flip our wonder switches back on.[17]

But what if you're reading this as someone who hasn't had a traumatic experience? According to the National Council for Behavioral Health, 70 percent of adults in the US have experienced some type of traumatic event at least once in their lives.[18] At this time of writing, that's approximately 229 million people, and a lot of crushed wonder. Even in the absence of trauma there exists a plethora of phobias and fears. What about all the other unhealthy fears that plague the activity of our creative imaginations?

If our experiences of trauma can crush our wonder, then facing our past and doing the inner work to heal can help us reclaim the wonder we've lost, course-correcting the creative work of our imagination. Doing this difficult, healing work will help us realize our own inner strength. We can't go back and change the pain of our past, but we do have the power to change our suffering, for our suffering is often in the story we create to make sense of our pain. Remember, you are the storyteller.

Two Words That Change Everything

Two of the most powerful words of the English language are "What if?"

"What if" is the foundation for countless stories. What if a giant killer shark terrorized a small town? I have a feeling Peter Benchley asked that question when he wrote *Jaws*. What if an alien race came to visit earth? Practically every sci-fi story is based on that question. What if a brave young woman volunteered to fight in an event with life-or-death stakes? Suzanne Collins answers this question in *The Hunger Games*. What if a crazed fan trapped a famous writer? Stephen King addressed this question in his book *Misery*. What if toys had feelings? What if fish had feelings? What if robots had feelings? What if feelings had feelings? "What if" is the birthplace of almost every Pixar film.

When you ask "what if?" you start to think and dream. These two words are vision-casting words—they invite you to look with wonder toward the future. You might even find yourself creating something new. "What if?" engages your brain to consider the many possibilities and to pursue wonder. "What if?" cracks open the door of possibility and invites passion and purpose in.

However, we often misplace our "what if?" mindset. Instead of applying this question to the present or the future, we apply it to the past. And this question eats at us from the inside. Asking "what if?" about the past gradually transforms to "if only."

If only I were more attractive, I would not be alone.

If only I were smarter, I would have more money.

If only I had worked harder, I would not have gotten fired.

"If only" will guide you to shame. Over time, as these shaming thoughts plague your mind, you will accept these lies as truth. A great way to avoid this pitfall is to turn your "what ifs" around and put them back where they belong: on your future, not your past. Unless the goal is to engage in a form of healing from previous trauma as in the research outlined earlier, practice using your imagination to look forward, not back.

The dark sides of our imaginations are powerful and can crush our wonder if we let them. If we give in to backward-looking "what ifs," we end up living in the past, constantly replaying the stories we've lived, thinking of all the ways we could have said or done things differently.

"What if I wouldn't have made that mistake?"

"What if I wouldn't have said those words?"

But what's done is done. While you can't control the past, it can inform the present and be used to predict the future. If we're stuck, it can often be useful to go backward in order to move forward. But you have the opportunity to reimagine your future. When we reawaken our wonder, we're permitted to shift to forward-looking "what ifs" instead.

"What if I tried something new?"

"What if I wrote that book I've always wanted to write?"

"What if I started a business?"

"What if I asked her out?"

"What if I decided enough is enough and courageously chose myself?"

What does your future hold? Or better yet, what would you *like* for your future to hold? Can you visualize it? Just visualizing it alone increases the chances of that imagined future becoming a reality. As Henry David Thoreau wrote, "This world is but a canvas to our imagination."[19] It's time to paint on a blank canvas and stop trying to repaint over parts of your old ones.

If wonder gives you permission to believe in things you have yet to see as possible, what would it look like for you to dream with no limitations? Go ahead. Try it. Visualize the life of your dreams.

Seriously, I'm not kidding. Pause your reading. Close your eyes and imagine.

What does that life look like? Now write it down. Type it on an empty screen. Paint it on a blank canvas if you'd like. Some people have even created a wonder board, their version of a vision board, filled with magical, aspirational images that anchor your "what ifs" in the future.

If your wonder switch has grown old and rusty because it's been off for a while and you've been misusing your imagination for far too long, this kind of visualization might not come easily.

Shifting your mind's use of "if only" to "what if?" is going to take some time and practice, just like strengthening a muscle.

Maria Montessori, an Italian doctor, educator, and innovator who founded the now famous school and way of education known by the same name, said, "Imagination does not become great until human beings, given the courage and the strength, use it to create."[20] It is time to use your imagination to create in positive and productive ways. And the act of creating and innovating is not something reserved for a select few among us. You, regardless of the type of wonder work your vocation leads you to, can live a creative life filled with magic. That is, if your curiosity is greater than your fear.

"What if I fail?" you may wonder.

You might. And you will grow.

"But what if I continue to fail?"

What if you don't?

It's time to take action. It's time to put your wonder to work. By the time you're finished with this book, my hope is that you will feel able to choose and develop what I like to call a Wonder Mindset. A Limiting Mindset believes the best way to do anything is the way it's always been done. A Wonder Mindset never stops learning, growing, or creating. A Limiting Mindset believes the best is in the past. A Wonder Mindset believes we have only scratched the surface of what is possible. A Limiting Mindset is ruled by fear and worry. A Wonder Mindset permits you to believe in magic and will lead you to do the impossible.

CHAPTER 6

The Wonder Mindset

Aim for the Moon (and Beyond)

I once had a teacher in middle school tell me that our attitudes determine our actions. I later discovered that great leaders understand this well. So do great parents. It's possible to conform my kids' behavior by training them to repeatedly make certain choices that over time turn into habits. But that approach comes with a countdown clock. As they get older, they think more on their own, and they no longer bend to my will. They develop their own narrative based on their experiences. This narrative also shapes their mindsets, which become the primary drivers of their actions and behavior.

What is your current state of mind? Are you thinking for yourself or letting other people do it for you? Do you need to rewire your brain? It's more possible than most people realize. For example, I can't just tell my kids what to think; I have to teach them *how* to think. And in teaching them how to think, I can help them develop a certain kind of mindset.

This is why *moments* of wonder aren't enough to transform a life. If it's true and lasting change we're after, we have to develop a Wonder *Mindset*. We have to reorient the way we see the world, our starting point for understanding everything. In other words, we have to unlearn the limits and lies we've been trained to believe, rediscover our incredible capacity, and essentially rewire our brains.

A mindset is simply the attitude from which all our actions flow. If seeing isn't believing but believing is seeing, then what we believe to be true makes all the difference in the world. In this way, we can begin to understand that our mindset determines our behavior. It drives our decision-making and shapes our outlook on life.

Remember Henry Ford's famous words? "Whether you think you can or you think you can't, you're right." If you believe this idea is reality, then don't you want to get to a place where you constantly believe "you can"? Because if you can, well, then you often will. Your mindset can be viewed as what you believe is possible. If wonder gives us permission to believe in what we have yet to see, then the goal is to transition from a limited or fixed mindset to what I like to call a Wonder Mindset.

In her groundbreaking research and corresponding book *Mindset*, which now deservedly has over two million copies in print, Dr. Carol Dweck popularized the idea of having a mindset that is growth oriented and brought important attention to the differences between that and what she calls a "fixed mindset."

In my experience of speaking to tens of thousands of people live each year, and in the offstage conversations that follow those onstage keynotes, an overwhelming majority of people struggle with limiting beliefs—beliefs that come from an experience, like scar tissue that results from a wound. These limiting thoughts and beliefs give way to a fixed mindset, and when your mindset is fixed, so is your personal and professional development. You're left feeling stuck, like you have no options. Progress does not seem possible, so you are left settling for the status quo. Before long, you grow complacent and comfortably numb to the excitement you once felt in your dreams.

Have you ever found yourself in that place? I know I have. It's exactly how I felt during all the seasons of life when my wonder switch was off.

One of the reasons many of us struggle with our fixed mindsets is because we believe the lie that our talent and intelligence are fixed traits. We believe our IQ has a ceiling. While we might be able to develop our natural talents, we think the capacity for growth in those areas is fixed. We conclude that our limits are determined at birth either by fate or by intelligent design or are outside our control and are left up to serendipitous alchemy.

Do we have limitations? Of course! I do. You do. We all do. But there is a huge gap between where you currently are and the upper bounds of human limitation. Many of your limiting beliefs don't make sense in light of the truth about what you are capable of. And far too often, we've allowed others to tell us what we can or can't do, instead of deciding for ourselves.

We put human beings on the moon. Are you aiming for something crazier than that? Probably not. Yet that was human achievement over five decades ago. Why not aim for more? Yes, "You can be whatever you want!" is probably a stretch. But there is a disparity between what you currently believe you can do and what you can actually do.

Dweck's research beautifully outlines this concept and walks us through the challenges we face when we believe the common assumption that intelligent people are simply born smart. She writes, "If you have only a certain amount of intelligence, a certain personality, and a certain moral character—well, then you'd better prove that you have a healthy dose of them. It simply wouldn't do to look or feel deficient in these most basic characteristics."[1]

This kind of mindset can leave us trying to put all our hope in the cards we've been dealt, which will only leave us feeling frustrated that we weren't dealt the hand we wish we would have been.

Dweck continues, "I've seen so many people with this one consuming goal of proving themselves—in the classroom, in their careers, and in their relationships. Every situation calls for a confirmation of their intelligence, personality, or character. Every situation is evaluated: Will I succeed or fail? Will I look smart or dumb? Will I be accepted or rejected? Will I feel like a winner or a loser?"[2]

If you can relate to these feelings or if this has ever been your mindset in the past, you know it's an exhausting state of mind. Instead of growing, you spend your time measuring. Instead of stepping outside your comfort zone and risking the judgment of others, you play it safe to ensure that you won't be challenged and, therefore, decrease your risk of failure.

But the beautiful part of Dweck's research is that we don't have to live with the hand of cards we've been dealt. We have the ability to develop our hand, throw away some cards every now and then, get some new ones, and learn how to better play the game by learning and growing along the way. When you have a Wonder Mindset, the hand you're dealt is just the starting point, and from there you have nowhere to go but up. Dweck asks,

> Why waste time proving over and over again how great you are, when you could keep getting better? Why hide deficiencies instead of overcoming them? Why look for friends or partners

who will just shore up your self-esteem instead of ones who will also challenge you to grow? And why seek out the tried and true, instead of experiences that will stretch you? The passion for stretching yourself and sticking to it, even (or especially) when it's not going well, is the hallmark of the growth mindset. This is the mindset that allows people to thrive during some of the most challenging times in their lives.[3]

Mic drop.

This is where we begin to see the difference between two mindsets: the Limiting Mindset and the Wonder Mindset. A Limiting Mindset is one that places limits on what is possible. In contrast, a Wonder Mindset is driven by wonder and promotes growth. A Wonder Mindset allows you to see and know that opportunities are everywhere.

A Wonder Mindset is one that believes you are moldable and malleable—that you can be developed and that the primary way you are developed is through the ways you are challenged. There's a difference between a Wonder Mindset and simply believing you're talented. Of course you're talented. But believing in your talents, or even saying, "Believe in yourself," is not the same as believing you can do anything you want, based on your willingness to learn and develop. Even if you feel like you're not as talented as others, which is most likely a limiting belief rooted in lies, you always have the opportunity to grow and step up your game by learning new skills.

Dweck echoes this duality in *Mindset*:

We often see books with titles like *The Ten Secrets of the World's Most Successful People* crowding the shelves of bookstores, and these books may give us many useful tips. But the world's most successful people still have their secrets. Instead, as you begin to understand the fixed and growth mindsets, you will see exactly how one thing leads to another—how a belief that your qualities are carved in stone leads to a host of thoughts and actions, and how a belief that your qualities can be cultivated leads to a host of different thoughts and actions, taking you down an entirely different road.[4]

At the heart of this idea of developing a Wonder Mindset is realizing that to be awake to wonder means to be a learner. Being a learner means placing a high value on growth and perspective. You were not "born this way." You can change. You can develop your talents, skills, and abilities. You can grow. Your limiting beliefs can be changed. Just because you're not good at something today doesn't mean you won't be good at something tomorrow. An old dog *can* learn new tricks.

Sadly, there are people reading or listening to this right now who will never live the life they were put on this earth to live, simply because they don't believe it's possible. Don't be one of those people. A Wonder Mindset is the key that unlocks the doors to wonderland and the magical life that perhaps up until now you've only dreamed of.

So how do we flip from a Limiting Mindset to one that is filled with possibilities? A great place to begin might be the opposite of what you'd expect.

Give Yourself Permission to Be Average

The first step to claiming a Wonder Mindset is embracing the truth that you are average. That is not a typo. Those may not be words you'd expect to read in a book about wonder and possibility, but they can free your mind and permit your wonder switch to be flipped on in magical ways. Regardless of what self-help gurus try to tell you, or what well-intentioned parents may have tried to lead you to believe, you were not born extraordinary. The truth is, most of us aren't. Even the people you think are extraordinary usually aren't—you're usually just judging them by their high-light reels. A look behind the curtain might give you a different impression.

The good news is, with a Wonder Mindset, average is enough—enough to accomplish almost anything you want. Our mindset has to do with what we build our identity on, and a lot of us root our identities in the approval of others, so we "put on a show," as we discussed earlier. We must learn to root our identity in something far less fragile than the applause of others. Otherwise, if you live for the approval of others, their rejection will kill you. History says that Jesus, one of the most famous people who ever lived, was welcomed with a parade of praise when he came to the city of Jerusalem. But the crowd who bowed at his feet and cheered was the same crowd who asked the government to execute him less than a week later. Crowds are fickle. Trying to please the mob is a never-ending chess match driven by comparison.

I'm sure you've heard the saying that "comparison is the thief of joy."[5] A belief that you were born average gives you permission to stop comparing yourself with others, robbing you of your joy, and permits you to believe you have the same cards to play with as everyone else. We want to put ourselves in situations where we excel and easily succeed, because it boosts our self-esteem, but we don't grow in those situations. Can you, an average human being, live an extraordinary life? Absolutely.

Position Yourself for Growth

Just last week a friend and mentor texted to check in and ask how I was doing while I navigated some large projects and opportunities coming down the pipeline. I didn't know how to reply other than to merely say, "I have no idea what I'm doing. I feel like I'm just making it up as I go." He proceeded to explain that this was a very good thing because it meant I was positioned for growth. He comforted me by letting me in on a secret: all innovators, creative thinkers, and great leaders "make it up as they go." He spent most of his career as a longtime respected creative leader at Nike doing the same. Don't let your Limiting Mindset fool you into thinking you're the only one who doesn't have it all figured out.

When you position yourself for growth, instead of "guaranteed" success by taking the easy path, you're going to feel challenged; often you'll feel like you don't know what you're doing. The wonder switch makes this possible because your curiosity becomes greater than your fear and the possibility of learning becomes more important than the consequences of failure—consequences that are often misperceived as being far more threatening than they actually are.

Out of your depth? Excellent. In over your head? Even better. Congratulations: you are now positioned for growth.

Praise the Process

There's a phrase that has infiltrated our culture and is consistently repeated in Twitter timelines and Instagram captions all over the internet: "Give others grace. We're all doing our best." I understand the heart behind this idea, and grace should never be in short supply. But "we're all doing our best"? Are we really? I'm not sure I buy it, unless what we're all doing our best at is making excuses to validate the untrue stories we're telling ourselves.

Let's be brutally honest with ourselves. A lot of us aren't doing our best. Most people may not be intentionally giving *less* than they're capable of, but a lot of us are barely scraping the surface of our true human potential. The problem is not in our ability or natural talent but in whether we value failure and learning.

Somewhere along the way, we have equated struggling with doing our best. We've come to believe that if it's hard, then surely our capacity is capped out. A Limiting Mindset gives birth to these kinds of lies by saying, "Well, I didn't succeed, but because I gave it my best, that must mean it just isn't meant to be." Then our subconscious kicks into overdrive, leading us to make choices and take actions that justify the lies as truth.

A Wonder Mindset says, "Well, I didn't succeed . . . yet. Even though I failed, I am capable of learning and growth, so my 'best' can always get better."

Learning to add the word *yet* to our assessment of our achievements gives us permission to grow and helps us maintain a Wonder Mindset.

"I can't" becomes "I haven't . . . yet."

Adding *yet* gives us permission to keep going, keep trying, and keep exploring ways of learning. Adding *yet* also leads us to a key component of the Wonder Mindset: the willingness to fail. We must embrace failure as a form of growth.

The harsh reality is you're never going to succeed in all you aspire to do. Chasing the right-sized dream guarantees a struggle, but it does not guarantee success. But in the struggle lies your becoming. Success is a poor teacher, but failure accelerates learning. The bigger you dream, the more you will fail. The more you fail, the more you can learn and grow.

Carol Dweck validates this idea by encouraging readers of her book to "praise the process." It is in the process, not in the successful crossing of the finish line, that the magic lies. The process is where the insights are. It offers us perspective and wisdom. This is the danger that comes with the "we're all doing our best" mentality. It's a mentality that settles for complacency. We are all in process of living, by default. But many of us are coasting.

Let's say you want to get in better shape and overall health. Are you challenging yourself when you exercise, or are you merely showing up? If you want to grow your business, are you reaching out to potential customers or clients personally, or are you simply posting more average content online in hopes of a response? Maybe you want to improve your craft, start a new hobby, or get a better job. Are you trying new things, or are you just doing things the way they've always been done?

The answers to these questions matter. Are you coasting, or are you pedaling? Pedaling gets you better results. But the result may not be "success." The results should be measured by two simple questions: What did I learn? And how did I grow as a result of the struggle? If your natural response to that question is, "I didn't struggle," then you're not trying hard enough. Situations that don't require you to struggle are ones that don't require your best.

Far too often failure crushes our wonder when it could teach us the way of resilience. Failure doesn't have to shut us down. Rather, failure can make us *stronger* by inviting us to keep practicing our try-again muscle. How do we keep our struggles and failure from turning our wonder switch off? We need to explore our relationship with failure. The stories of our failures often hold the keys to unlock the obstacles to wonder.

Our mindset is a difference maker because it affects how we view failure and, more importantly, how we respond to failure. It all comes back to our beliefs and what they permit us to see beyond what we experience in the present.

The pain we experience in the present often causes us to think, "Ouch, that hurt." Our brains tell us, "Make the pain stop." No one enjoys pain, but it is an amazing teacher and motivator.

As I was writing this chapter, my four-year-old daughter, Everly, came into the room with a frown on her face, saying she needed a Band-Aid. She had been outside playing and fell down, scraping an arm and a leg. After I picked her up and consoled her, I asked about what happened. My second question was simply, "What happened after you fell down?" "I got back up," she said. And that's what we do when we fail. We get back up. And the pain we feel as we get back up reminds us to change our behavior.

I praised my daughter's effort, hoping it will enable her to continue developing a Wonder Mindset as she grows up. Being brave will permit her to embrace challenges along the way instead of always playing it safe. The result will not always mean she succeeds at everything she sets out to do, but it does mean she will set out to do more than she would have otherwise. Her failures may still hurt. We all need a bandage from time to time, but our failures don't have to define us. We can fail without being a failure.

One of the most valuable lessons I've learned about failure is to lean into it. I tend to worry, so I handle failure by embracing it. I ask myself, "Okay, what's the worst that can happen?"

Often the answer is not as bad as the extreme scenarios my mind likes to create. While you may remember your failures like they are etched in permanent marker on your bathroom mirror, others tend to forget them. They will often admire your perseverance instead.

So how exactly does one make the switch from a Limiting Mindset to a Wonder Mindset? By practice. When we practice better habits, we create better neural pathways. And this is the best news for us all: we *can* rewire our brains for the life we hope to live.

Your Plastic Brain

Your brain is incredible, which is why we were all told not to do drugs as kids. When I was in elementary school, the "this is your brain on drugs" commercials on TV were always accompanied by an egg frying in a skillet. It's an effective metaphor, and the storytellers who wrote those commercials knew it.

I'm not sure if it was because of the antidrug campaigns and commercials, but drugs never appealed to me as a kid. What I wanted was a mind with magic powers. And I'm not alone. Our society never seems to get enough of mind readers, fortunetellers, and horoscopes, regardless of the never-ending research that invalidates the psychic industry as a whole. It should come as no surprise that even the industry I am part of as a professional illusionist is filled with gurus and shamans who pilfer our training and resources for fresh ways to con and swindle. What's surprising is not that deception occurs but that the deception runs so deep that even those doing the deceiving convince themselves that their powers are real.

The reality is, we don't need a horoscope that looks to the stars for answers and magic. We can instead look to the same miraculous magic that made the stars and realize that even some of the dust that makes up the stars that fall across the galaxy makes up part of us.[6] Once you dig into the ways that science backs that up, is it so far-fetched to believe in the magical powers you already have? You've already been hardwired with magic. Remember, that doesn't make you special. That makes you average—every human being shares this design. You were not designed with the power to know or predict the future. You were designed with the power to create the future.

Just a few decades ago, scientists believed that significant changes in the brain could take place only between infancy and childhood, which means by the time you stepped into adulthood, the concrete form of your brain's physical structure had been set. Talk about a fixed mindset! But this doesn't have to do with only your IQ. By the 1960s researchers had become intrigued by cases of older adults who had suffered strokes but were able to regain functioning of parts of their bodies. Researchers started to question whether the brain was perhaps more malleable (plastic) than previously assumed.

But our brains don't just rewire themselves from the damage caused by strokes or other forms of trauma. We can also actively rewire our brains and, in turn, redesign our lives.

The more neuroscientists venture into the design and intricacies of the human brain, the more groundbreaking discoveries there are to confirm that our brains have the ability to change based on our experiences. And in this plasticity lies additional potential for changing our beliefs that inform our behavior. Our repeated behavior forms habits by creating new neural pathways.

Your brain is composed of approximately eighty-five billion neurons. Neurons are the cells in your nervous system. As you go about your day, these neurons talk to each other in all sorts of ways.

Think of them as the "basic working unit of the brain—a specialized cell designed to transmit information to other nerve cells, muscle, or gland cells."[7] Eighty-five billion may sound like a lot of neurons—and it is—but we now know that neurogenesis, the creation of new neurons, doesn't stop at birth. If you are able to create new neurons, change the way the neurons you already have "talk to each other" by forming new connections, and change the pathways those neurons travel by creating new habits, you essentially possess the ability to rewire your brain. Suddenly, changing your mindset, behavior, and habits is not remotely out of the question. If you can rewire your brain, you have the ability to revive your wonder and to reimagine your life.

Research points to two types of neuroplasticity. The first is "functional plasticity," which the American Psychological Association defines as "the ability of the brain to adapt to loss of or damage to tissue by transferring all or part of the functions previously performed by those injured areas to other regions."[8] This is the type of plasticity related to regaining functioning after a stroke. This plasticity is truly incredible and good news for us all, but our focus for the subject at hand is on a second type—"structural plasticity," which is the brain's ability to change its physical structure in response to what we learn.

Despite your brain's having billions of neurons, if they don't form the right connections with one another and with other structures in your brain, they will eventually die. And though plasticity exists into adulthood, neuron loss is a natural part of aging and brain development. But every time you learn something new, your brain replaces some of the neurons you've lost and builds connections among the ones you have. But what is required to learn something new and start that process?

In chapter 5 we briefly touched on the power of visualization. Developing a mindset that is driven by wonder is key to leveraging the true power of your imagination. And you can use that imagination to tangibly rewire your brain through visualization.

In 2003, Alvaro Pascual-Leone, a neuroscientist at Harvard Medical School, rounded up a group of volunteers and brought them into the lab to play the piano. They began with a five-finger piano exercise, asking one group to practice for two hours per day, every day, for five days. At the end of each day's exercise, the participants took a test. A "transcranial-magnetic-stimulation" was performed, which involved taking a coil of wire and running it across the top of their heads from ear to ear and sending a short magnetic pulse into the motor cortexes of their brains. Doing so allowed the researchers to look at the function of neurons. What they discovered came as no surprise. As a specific muscle was used more, the volunteers' brains devoted more real estate to its development. But this part of the study was simply to find a point of comparison for what would come next.

Another group of participants were asked merely to think. That's it, just think about the same piano exercise, practicing only in their minds. They didn't need to move their fingers—they didn't even need a piano. They would play the exact same piece of music in their heads, simply imagining how they would move their fingers. When the same transcranial-magnetic-stimulation test was performed, the region of the motor cortex that controls the piano-playing fingers expanded in the brains of volunteers who only imagined playing the music, the same way it did in the brains of those who had actually played it.[9] What we think or imagine has the ability to form connections that we can later put into practice in reality, outside of the land of "make-believe."

This discovery was validated by a study by Australian psychologist Alan Richardson, who gathered a group of basketball players who had never practiced visualization and tested each player's ability to make free throws.

The first group practiced every day for twenty days. The second group practiced only on the first and last days of the twenty-day study. The third group also practiced only on the first and last days but also spent twenty minutes visualizing their free throws every day in between. At this point, you can probably guess the results. The significant improvement was in the third group who practiced visualization by imagining their movements and shots and the balls hitting nothing but net. They didn't just improve; they showed almost the same level of improvement as the first group who physically practiced all twenty days.

To some, this feels almost like magic. And maybe it is, but it's not the woo-woo kind; it's the real kind, backed by science. That our brains are so powerful may seem far-fetched, but it's the way they're wired. And because of that, you have more power to rewire your brain than you might realize. The house I'm sitting in right now was already wired when I bought it. But it has since been transformed through the process of renovation, and that included completely rewiring it. The rewiring and renovation were parts of transforming our house into the home we imagined.

Your body—including your brain—will default to relying on what it already knows. But if you create new neural pathways and strengthen them through repetition, you introduce the opportunity to form new habits that can dramatically alter the life you're living.

Be careful not to fall for the neuroplasticity hype, as many self-proclaimed gurus have set out to sell visualization and other facets of neuroplasticity as the ultimate wonder drug. Just as we discovered with the placebo effect and the power of suggestion earlier in this book, as powerful and effective as neuroplasticity is, sometimes the proper course of action is to go see a doctor.

Practicing Visualization

Through visualization, you have the power to make much of what is imaginable, tangible, because your brain can't always distinguish between a memory and the future you are imagining and building a story around.[10] Practicing visualization strengthens the neural pathways and connections necessary in your brain. So rather than focusing on the challenges and hurdles that get in your way and hold you back, imagine what you want to see instead. The new pathways and connections will give way to beliefs that will change what you see in "reality."

Obviously, visualizing crossing a finish line alone will not get you across it, because attaining a goal still requires putting in the effort. But the finish line will be nearly impossible to cross if you can't visualize it at all. If you can't see yourself attaining what you aspire to achieve, you won't achieve it. Because "whether you think you can or you can't, you're right." The "thought" of what is possible or impossible must become a practice of regular visualization.

To be clear, prior to the practice of visualization, we need an actual experience to improve upon. That practice is then reinforced through visualization. If I've never taken a skydiving lesson or received some kind of instruction, merely visualizing what I'm going to do when I jump out of the plane will not lead to a story with a very happy ending. Instruction from a professional combined with visualization would lead to a far more successful experience. And while visualization is popular among athletes, it's relevant to every part of our lives.

Everything I've written about in this book has been put into practice while I've written it. This book would not have gotten finished without maintaining a Wonder Mindset. Some days I sat down to write but failed to find the words, and through that failure, I grew. The struggles allowed me to evaluate, learn, and pivot along the way. Embracing the risk of failure becomes a consistent opportunity for growth as a writer. But the ways a Wonder Mindset helped me didn't stop there.

Having a Wonder Mindset gave me permission to practice visualization in ways that fueled my creative process. But I haven't just visualized the words; I had to write them. Wonder gave me permission to believe in the possibility of becoming a bestselling author with the ability to help tens of thousands of people through the ideas in this book, which gave me the ability to imagine it. Using my imagination to practice visualization, I have almost daily closed my eyes and visualized what being a bestselling author might look like, including visualizing opening a web browser and reading the five-star reviews on Amazon. I have visualized the call from Margaret, my literary agent, letting me know I hit a bestseller list. I have visualized emcees at live events who will be adding, "Please welcome bestselling author . . ." to their onstage introductions. As I do that, my heart rate increases. My legs power up with the anticipation of walking on stage. This shows that the visualization is not just in the prefrontal cortex of my brain but lives in the limbic system. It's alive in the part of my brain that is outside conscious awareness.

Why do I visualize these things? Is it because being a bestselling author with an ego fed by hundreds of five-star reviews is my idea of success? I'll be the first to admit that the thought of receiving five-star reviews and being a bestselling author is exciting. But what drives me is what drives us all—the desire for meaning and purpose. Instead of being a sign of "success," a five-star review says to me, "Yes, this book offered me value. And I want others to know about it so it can impact their lives as well."

Obviously, visualizing those five-star reviews will not guarantee them. But visualizing allows my brain to do the work of filling in the words that would accompany those reviews, words that explain the ways that my own words have impacted the stories of others. This forms new pathways for the neurons in my brain to travel on, decreasing the roadblocks that place limits on my potential as a thinker, writer, and human being, leading me and enabling me to do the work of developing the habits necessary to cross the finish line.

Practicing Awareness

I once heard entrepreneur Tom Bilyeu say, "Beliefs, habits, routines, values—these are the things that make up someone."[11]

I'm not sure I'd oversimplify the totality of who we are by saying we are made up of only those four things, but our beliefs, habits, routines, and values certainly shape the experience of our lives. This brings up a valuable question: What is the relationship between beliefs and habits? Which comes first?

When you develop a Wonder Mindset, your brain permits you to make new choices. The old, untrue stories you've been telling yourself are now questioned, which gives way to wonder and the creation of new stories. As that happens, your brain starts to work less on validating the old story, and your curiosity starts to beckon you to choices that support the new one. Those new choices, repeated over time, form the habits that shape the trajectory of your life. This process will take you to a place where you are invited to take responsibility to sustain your wonder and the new story accompanying it.

In other words, if you want to reimagine your future, it's time to take responsibility for the life you've lived so far.

This is not as simple as it seems at the surface, but you're living the life you have designed in an effort to survive the narrative that has been created and adopted, all in response to the lies you were tricked into believing.

We have to take responsibility for our decisions. You can't control other people. You can't control the rest of the world. There are certainly facets of your own life that are outside your control, and the level of control we think we possess in other areas is often another illusion. But we do have the power to wake up each morning and to express control over our lives through our repeated choices: our habits.

Again, the writing of this book has forced me to practice what I'm preaching here. I've heard other authors somewhat jokingly say, "Just be careful when you set out to write a book. You're going to have to live out your message." I now know what they meant on a deeper level than I did before. I have learned that if you set out to write a book about wonder, seemingly everything in the entire universe is going to feel like it's waging war on your wonder.

There was a time about halfway through this book when I wanted to give up. A combination of fear, doubt, and worry crept in. My Wonder Mindset that I had worked years to develop began to crack and chip away. The dark side of my imagination that I had spent so long holding at bay came like a thief in the night, ransacking my wonderland, trying to steal my optimism. What happened?

This wasn't the first time the world had conspired against my wonder, but this time I had developed character, core values, faith, and beliefs. Healthier habits, greater awareness, and routines and rituals gave me everything I needed to weather the storm. And storms will always come. You don't always know when or how or from where, but they will indeed come. Your mindset will either raise or lower your chances of surviving those storms with your wonder still awake.

At the core of keeping my wonder alive—not only in times of smooth sailing but also when the waves came crashing in—was awareness. For the first time in my life, I had developed enough self-awareness to at least be more fully present and tuned in to the magic. Magic is not as visible in a storm, but it's always there, doing its work, keeping you going, as long as you're paying attention.

Paying attention is something that has come up more than once throughout this book, but it isn't a simple task. Then again, let's be honest—very little of what we've covered so far falls into the category of "simple."

I once had a mentor explain that the goal of life is to "wake up." I eventually learned that this meant being not only physically awake but also fully aware—present and tuned in. But tuning in and seeing clearly are hard when so many things cloud our judgment. That's why you must develop the ability to be fully aware. When the storms come, the clouds will be thick and the rain will be heavy. You won't be able to see what's in front of you. But with wonder present, you often see most clearly when your eyes are closed.

One of the greatest lessons I've learned so far in this less-than-four-decades-long life is closing my eyes to see. This approach allows me to disconnect from the triggers of my environment and close off my five physical senses. I can then focus on what is capturing my focus and attention. When I'm aware, I can offer a conscious response as an intentional act toward healthier beliefs and habits. These are part of the essential foundation that propels you from an old story to a new story.

So how do we become aware? How do we then act on our awareness? Doing so requires developing a regular practice of mindfulness. With the rise in guided meditation apps, many have confused mindfulness with meditation. A regular practice of meditation can assist with mindfulness, but mindfulness is also simply one of many ways to meditate. That said, I think it's incredibly difficult to practice mindfulness without making meditation a habit-shaping daily ritual. This activity is essential to keeping your wonder switch turned on. Human beings have around sixty to seventy thousand thoughts per day. And remember, just because you have a thought doesn't make it true. The more mindful you are of those thoughts, the less chance they will slip by your awareness unchecked. If they do, they will turn your wonder switch off.

Being mindful is about tuning out the distractions that come from doing, so you can learn to be present and really be. After all, as is commonly said, you are a human being, not a human doing. When you learn how to really be, you can become mindful and comfortable with the uncomfortable thoughts and feelings that lead you to distract yourself in the first place. You have to unlearn before you can relearn and return to your original state of wonder.

The word *meditation* means "to become familiar with." As you become familiar with the untrue stories you're telling yourself, you can respond by exposing those stories as lies. Ironically, it's through practices like meditation that you gain greater understanding of the truth—the thing that those who value certainties and absolutes are so in search of.

It appears that most people are not participating in any kind of meditation or mindfulness practice. In research for this book, one survey of more than two hundred participants showed that only 35 percent of people set aside time each day for reflection or meditation. Yet in this same survey, over 73 percent of those same participants said they enjoy learning new things through random exploration. And 75 percent said they wanted to be more open to new possibilities. The research shows an obvious gap between our aspirations and the practices necessary to attain those aspirations.

Meditation is a helpful practice, but developing mindfulness is not limited to the act of meditation. I have grown to think of mindfulness more as an approach to living, not something you do only when you sit and close your eyes to meditate. You can practice mindfulness any time, wherever you are, throughout your day by being fully present and engaged. Some would call this living a more contemplative life, and contemplation comes in various forms. It's nearly impossible to be contemplative throughout our lives without the presence of wonder.

As we become more awake *and* aware, we increase our ability to hold on to our Wonder Mindset when experiences outside our control trigger lies and limiting beliefs that can rob us of the wonder that makes this mindset possible in the first place. Learning to pay attention to the parts of our story and interactions with the stories of others that trigger those lies and limiting beliefs is an integral part of becoming awake and aware. This includes the triggers from the environment around us, which is why the environments you live and work in are key to keeping your wonder switch turned on. They are so important, in fact, they're the focus of our next chapter.

But before we venture off into wonderland, let's take a moment to explore the practice of being mindful of your limiting beliefs. As you become more tuned in and fully present, you'll notice more internal conflict between your old story and your new story. That conflict exists at the intersection between the two stories: the old stories, which your brain is trying to hold on to and justify as true, and wonder, which is saying, "No, you may not have seen the new story unfold yet, but I am giving you permission to believe that story is possible." That's when limiting beliefs kick in, attempting to fix your attitude on driving actions that grip you with fear to keep you safe. Don't buy the lies.

How do you respond to those lies and limiting beliefs that sneak in and try to rob you of your Wonder Mindset? How do you react when a Limiting Mindset creeps back in? Begin by pressing pause and reflecting. When you feel like you're failing, for example, or when something you've set out to attain doesn't feel possible, press pause. Stop, reflect, and become mindful of the reality of the moment. Reflect on the situation from an objective reality instead of a subjective one. Ask yourself, "Where is this story coming from?"

Is your imagination playing tricks on you again? Is the source of your fear legitimately placing you in danger at that moment, or is it irrational fear, driven by a previous inciting incident earlier in your life? Is there any supporting evidence for or proof that the story you're telling yourself is true?

Much of the process of healing from trauma includes developing the ability to respond to something that happened in your story by saying, "That experience of pain occurred, and we acknowledge that while it indeed happened, it is not happening now." If this is something you are struggling with, I can relate. A qualified professional trained in experiential therapy is the best path toward healing.

As you become more grounded in the truth, it becomes more possible to identify the lie or lies you're telling yourself. You can work to identify the parts of the story that aren't true. Identify the trigger that led to the lie so you can develop a habit of recognizing the lie more quickly and easily in the future when that story creeps back in.Once you've paused, reflected, and identified the untrue parts of the story your limiting belief is holding on to, you can work on responding to your limiting beliefs with the truth. Again, depending on the inciting incident that your limiting beliefs are tied to, it may be necessary to participate in a corrective experience guided by a professional therapist or counselor. Even if considered not necessary, it would absolutely be helpful.

Maintaining a Wonder Mindset, once developed, can be assisted through the repetition of beliefs. Some people call these "affirmations," which may feel weird to others. I like to think of these affirmations of truth as reminders. It doesn't matter what you call them; it just matters that you identify the truth and repeat it. Say these truths out loud in response to the lies. Write them on your bathroom mirror with a dry-erase marker. Put them on sticky notes on your computer monitor at work. And it never hurts to affirm others as a way of helping them take back their power as well. I keep a dry-erase marker in one of the drawers of our bathroom vanity because I love leaving notes on our mirror that show my belief in my wife, and she loves it too.

In a culture that seems to have developed a love affair with these types of affirmations, hoping to use them as a shortcut, I feel that it's important to note that affirmations are only useful to reinforce and remind us of what is true, once we have gone through the healing process of moving from an old story to a new one.

Writing "I am enough" on my bathroom mirror and reading and repeating it to myself out loud every morning isn't going to change my life if that's all I'm doing to counteract the lies. That top-down process is not how our brains work. It may even end up doing more harm than good. "I'm *not* enough" was born out of the experience of trauma, and if I do not heal from that experience, affirmations merely become the equivalent of shouting truths into the wind, blown around by lies with no hope of landing in my heart.

Once you take the journey toward truth and healing, remind yourself of that truth and affirm it for yourself and for others. Then, and only then, will your Wonder Mindset start to develop, and your limiting beliefs begin to fade.

Practicing Gratitude

A practical way of developing awareness is through a habit of journaling. Journaling is an effective way of *practicing* awareness instead of just *gaining* awareness. As you gain awareness, you record it, which allows you to reflect on it. You can then frequently repeat the truths you discover and use that new awareness to identify necessary shifts and changes to the story you're setting out to live. This practice also presents an incredible opportunity for gratitude, one of the final key components of a Wonder Mindset.

"Something as simple as writing down three things you're grateful for every day for 21 days in a row significantly increases your level of optimism, and it holds for the next six months. The research is amazing," Harvard researcher and author Shawn Achor said in an interview with *Inc.* magazine.[12] Achor's studies on gratitude are amazing, and the neuroscience they reveal suggests so much about the seemingly magical power of gratitude.

In his book *What Happy People Know*, Dan Baker writes, "During active appreciation, the threatening messages from your amygdala [the fear center of the brain] and the anxious instincts of your brainstem are cut off, suddenly and surely, from access to your brain's neocortex, where they can fester, replicate themselves, and turn your stream of thoughts into a cold river of dread. It is a fact of neurology that the brain cannot be in a state of appreciation and a state of fear at the same time. The two states may alternate, but are mutually exclusive."[13]

If gratitude can take you out of a state of fear and worry, that means it also enables you to properly use your imagination to be productive in positive, creative, life-giving ways. This alone can inspire you to develop a regular practice of gratitude and shows why it is an essential part of the Wonder Mindset.

Try it out. Pause right now and name three things you're grateful for. Are you breathing? Do you have a roof over your head? If it's helpful, start with the basics and then move on from there. The more you become aware, the greater your list will grow. As part of my regular practice of journaling, I acknowledge three things I'm grateful for almost every day. Doing so has had a dramatic effect on my ability to cultivate a life of wonder and magic.

Limiting beliefs may currently rule your mindset, but you have the power to change those beliefs through the practice of visualization, awareness, journaling, and more. These habits and daily rituals serve as sparks that activate and sustain your wonder, keeping your wonder switch on.

If the world is robbing you of wonder, or you're doing the robbing yourself and falling prey to a Limiting Mindset, you can take back your power. You are powerful beyond measure. I like the way Marianne Williamson communicates this idea in her book, *Return to Love*: "Our deepest fear is not that we are inadequate. Our deepest fear is that we are powerful beyond measure. It is our light, not our darkness that most frightens us. We ask ourselves, 'Who am I to be brilliant, gorgeous, talented, fabulous?' Actually, who are you *not* to be? You are a child of God. Your playing small does not serve the world. There is nothing enlightened about shrinking so that other people won't feel insecure around you. We are all meant to shine, as children do."[14]

I have grown to a place where I am no longer comfortable playing small. A Wonder Mindset permits me to operate from a place of healthy power and strength. Won't you join me? The world needs you to stop shrinking and step into the life you were meant to live, not because we need you to rule over us but because we need your magic. And as you let your magic shine, you will give others permission to release their magic into the world as well.

This is usually the point where many teachers in the personal development space lean on your "power" as the source of all transformation. And while I believe in the "power within," I also understand that this power is a gift, and not all will receive that gift, own it, or steward it wisely.

My hope is that through the words of this book, you can develop a Wonder Mindset that changes your life. I hope the power that wonder carries is also demystified to a point of practicality, leaving you unintimidated by the process of changing your life. It really is that simple in concept. But don't let this simplicity let you lose sight of the magic that makes it possible. The power of a mindset driven by wonder can lead you, an average human being, to live an extraordinary life.

CHAPTER 7

Creating Wonderland

Your Environment Can
Change Your Life

You don't have to fall down a rabbit hole like Alice did to spend time in wonderland. You can create your own wonderland wherever you are, and doing so is one of the key components of sustaining your wonder by keeping the switch turned on.

In the previous chapter, we discovered how our mindset largely determines our choices and behavior and even how we see. Another way of saying that is that your attitude determines your actions. In this chapter, we explore how your attitude is often most shaped by your atmosphere—the environments you live and work in.

Outside of the obvious definition of the envelope of gases surrounding the earth, another definition of *atmosphere* is "the pervading tone or mood of a place, situation, or work of art." What atmosphere do you currently find yourself in? What is the pervading tone or mood of the places and situations you spend most of your time in? And what is the culture that has been created within those spaces?

Imagine being with those astronauts headed toward the moon. How would the atmosphere they were in impact their attitudes? Imagine the doubts, the fears, and all the other thoughts going through their minds as they sat in a rocket blasting off to outer space. The same wonder that led to their desire to go into space must have given them the ability to keep the dark side of their imaginations at bay, staying focused on the possibility of what could be.

But what happened as the atmosphere changed? What happened each time they ventured into a new space they hadn't been in before, until finally, they stepped out of a spaceship and onto the surface of the moon?

When your atmosphere changes, your mindset can change with it, because the environment you find yourself in is part of the story being told around you. Changing your environment alone may not turn on your wonder switch. But once the switch is flipped, your atmosphere is one of the primary factors that makes your wonder sustainable, keeping the switch in the on position and your Wonder Mindset intact. Likewise, the wrong atmosphere can snuff out your wonder.

By now it's possible that your imagination is being stirred in amazing ways and your curiosity is wild at work. But as you venture into the new story that serves as the next chapter of your life, it's important to understand that for wonder to be sustainable, you must perform an audit of the culture around you. Your environment should help you pursue magic through a state of wonder. If it doesn't, it will be very difficult to keep your wonder switch on. You'll be more likely to stay stuck and slip back into complacency.

To explore the power of atmospheres, think about the last experience you had where you left your day-to-day environment and entered a new atmosphere. It could have been a vacation to the beach or maybe the mountains. Or maybe it was a trip to Disneyland or even Las Vegas. Whether you're lying on a beach, sitting in a cabin staring at a range of mountains, or walking up and down Main Street in the "most magical place on earth," each of these environments has a profound impact on your attitude, for better or for worse.

Think about a casino in Las Vegas, for example. How much effort and intentionality can you assume has gone into creating the atmosphere needed for consumers to come inside, sit down, and spend as much time as possible playing inside a casino?

Maybe you're in the camp of people who can't stand casinos and therefore can't walk out of one fast enough. That also validates the power of an atmosphere. Whether an atmosphere is right or wrong for you, it can have a profound impact on the attitude that drives your behavior.

Psychology Today showcased a study that examined both cognitive satisfaction (whether the casino met the gambler's expectations) and affective satisfaction (the gambler's personal feelings of positive emotion). The research showed that cognitive satisfaction was most predicted by easy navigation of the space, ambience, and cleanliness of the space. Affective satisfaction was most predicted by easy navigation of the space, seating comfort, and interior decor.[1] All these factors are planned out and controlled by casinos to provide the best atmosphere.

Disney has similar priorities. It isn't just a magical place; it's quite possibly one of the cleanest places on earth. It is rare for a piece of trash that lands on the ground in a Disney park to remain there for more than a few minutes before a cast member picks it up and disposes of it. My three-year-old once accidentally missed the trash can at Magic Kingdom, and her drink cup tumbled to the ground. Before she had a chance to bend over and pick it up, a cast member had already not only bent down and thrown away the trash but also gotten down on one knee a second time and given her a sticker. What kid wouldn't want to spend as much time as possible in that kind of environment?

What great storytellers like Disney understand is that everything tells a story. The sights, the sounds, the smells—it all combines to form and contribute to the stories we tell ourselves. This idea is even baked into the stories that Disney's characters find themselves in. Ariel, the Little Mermaid, wanted to be part of a different world because the glimpses she got of that world sparked her wonder, piqued her curiosity, and influenced the story she told herself about who she wanted to be.

And what about in *Aladdin*? Princess Jasmine believed there had to be something more, something better, than simply following the steps of every royal who came before her. She felt constrained and trapped, believing that if she could just get free, she could be truly happy and seen. Aladdin gave her the opportunity to leave her constrained palace environment and took her on a magic carpet ride, showing her "a whole new world." Once she got a taste of the freedom and possibility she longed for, she was never the same. Her wonder was given wings, and it changed her narrative.

Great brands tell stories with their atmospheres on a regular basis. If you walk into an Apple Store, everything about the atmosphere they've created is designed to tell a story. Apple wows you with beautiful products showcased throughout their store. Although the store looks like an art gallery, you're invited in to come play with every product in the store and to experience the magic. Then the employees offer free hands-on magic lessons, opening your mind to the possibilities that exist with their products. The elegant experience doesn't leave you with just an understanding of how their products work. The brand is so strong that being part of the Apple community leads you to tell yourself a different story about who you are.

It isn't only multibillion-dollar companies that do this. Small businesses take advantage of these opportunities as well.

There's a famous mansion in Hollywood, California, known as the Magic Castle. For the members of the Academy of Magical Arts, a fraternity for magicians worldwide, the Magic Castle is considered our clubhouse. Perched on a hilltop a block off Hollywood Boulevard, the historical Victorian mansion is filled each evening with some of the best magicians in the world, as well as some of Hollywood's most notable celebrities. As you'd expect from a place called the Magic Castle, visiting is quite the experience, complete with secret doors, sliding bookcases, and endless amounts of magic being performed in nooks and crannies throughout.

Next door to the Magic Castle is a far less glamorous property known as the Magic Castle Hotel. Blink twice and you'll miss it. For starters, it doesn't even appear to be a hotel. It looks like a basic apartment building, not unlike many of the other apartment buildings in the area. Its humble appearance may leave a lot to be desired, but the hotel has developed a cult following among budget travelers and more. As a member of the Academy of Magical Arts and a regular visitor of the Magic Castle, I always saw the hotel next door but never considered staying there. Until I read the stories in the reviews.

At the time of this writing, the Magic Castle Hotel has over 2,500 five-star reviews on Tripadvisor, and out of hundreds of hotels listed on the site for Los Angeles, it is rated sixth overall.

One reviewer said, "This is the best hotel I've ever stayed in." Another said, "This may have been my best hotel experience in all of my travels." Dig deeper, and you begin to find out why.

"I hesitate to submit this review," one person said, "because once I do, this place will probably be booked for years. And well, it should be. The people who work there will absolutely reaffirm your faith in humanity." The curb appeal doesn't provide the perception of the fanciest hotel in Hollywood, and it certainly isn't a place where you're likely to catch a glimpse of a celebrity. But when you're treated like a celebrity and made to feel like a star, the magic of storytelling does its work.

What may now be the most well-known example of this magic is the hotel's complimentary service offerings. The hotel pool not only is open twenty-four hours a day but has a poolside phone known as the "popsicle hotline." Pick it up, request a flavor of your choice, and a butler will deliver your complimentary popsicle. Want another snack but are already back in your room? Pick up your phone and request chocolate, candy, chips, crackers, cookies, or popcorn. We aren't talking miniature Halloween candy—you'll receive full-size candy bars. Again, for free, twenty-four hours a day. Running short on clean clothes? Pick up your phone and a butler shows up at your door as part of the hotel's free laundry service.

When you experience that level of hospitality, it creates an atmosphere of wonder. You feel the magic, and it changes the story you tell yourself.

The Story around You

Whether you're at Disney World, a casino, an Apple Store, or the Magic Castle Hotel, your surroundings craft a story that can awaken your wonder. But what if you're not at a special place? What if you're somewhere uncomfortable?

A few years ago, we had the privilege of learning from an incredible presenter at STORY conference named Yoko Sen. She is a musician and sound engineer who spent many hours suffering in the hospital. While there, Yoko noticed the soundtrack of a hospital—the sounds of beeps and machines and workers—and how it all contributed to the atmosphere in which people were trying to heal from sickness and disease. Yoko described what it was like to know deep down that her life was finite, and every beep and every hushed tone made her feel that finality with deep fear and realism. She dared to ask the question, "What if?" and it changed her healing process.

In the same way that Leonardo da Vinci practiced observation, Yoko put her wonder to work by curiously exploring how she might transform hospital patients' sound experience. She wondered, "How can we make love audible and create a future that is more human?" That led to the creation of Sen Sound, which offers sound experiences designed to alleviate suffering.

Sen Sound embodies the truth of the research in chapter 4 on the neuroscience of awe and how wonder can help our bodies heal. It redesigns the atmosphere of a hospital by adjusting the sounds, which can change the stories the human brain tells itself about what is possible. Imagine a world in which intentional thought is given to things like sound design in a hospital room. Small changes like that can contribute to a sense of wonder and help put us in a headspace of peace and hope rather than fear. That imagined world is slowly becoming a reality, thanks to people like Yoko, who understand that atmosphere has a profound impact on our mindset.

The atmospheres of the environments you spend most of your time in have a profound impact on your wonder. I talk with many who struggle to shift their narrative. They desperately want to change the story they're telling themselves, leading to new habits and routines and possibilities, but haven't done the work to change their internal and external environments. The worlds they find themselves in just don't support or align with their aspirations.

Changing your life without changing your environment is like taking the character of Ariel in *The Little Mermaid* and putting her in Aladdin's desert world with no legs. That environment doesn't line up with the story of who Ariel is. Or take Jasmine and throw her into the sea. She doesn't have fins and isn't a mermaid, so she would drown. The character is stuck in the wrong environment, which only sets her up for failure.

What story do you want to live? What are your aspirations? Do you want to develop a healthier habit? Increase your income? Find more peace in your life? Create art that encourages others? Strengthen your bond with the people you love? A shift in atmosphere doesn't make these things happen. But intentionally designing an environment that supports your vision helps you experience magic and awaken your wonder. Inversely, if you spend a lot of time in an environment that doesn't support and sustain your dreams, your wonder switch may eventually be turned back off.

Once Jasmine went on a magic carpet ride, her wonder was given a new sense of life and vision. She already believed there had to be more, and allowing Aladdin to help her to see and touch it expanded her horizons. The stifling atmosphere of Agrabah's palace wasn't suitable for the story she had believed possible all along.

It's time to shift your perspective. What magic carpet ride do you need to go on to expand your horizons? It might be time for a whole new world.

Right in Front of You

One of the tricks I've become known for over the years is Paper Balls over the Head. A name like that doesn't leave much to the imagination. The trick is exactly what it sounds like, which doesn't sound very interesting in writing, but imagine this experience onstage.

You're at a magic show. You've experienced minds being magically read and objects mysteriously levitating. And then the magician asks for a volunteer. You join him onstage, with no idea of what is about to happen. You're invited to sit down in a chair and hold your hands in front of you, index fingers pointed at each other. The magician explains that he'll be testing your hand-eye coordination with a magical testing device, which he attaches to your fingers. The testing device? A roll of toilet paper, and you are now a human toilet paper holder.

What's going through your head? Drama. A lot of it. You do what any normal human being would do—focus on how everyone in the audience perceives you. "Do I look dumb right now? What's going on? Wait, I need to focus. He just said he was going to test my hand-eye coordination. But I have peers out in the audience watching me. I hope I don't end up looking like an idiot."

The magician then pulls off some toilet paper and wads it into a ball. He appears to place it in one of his hands. He then asks you to guess which one. You guess, but the paper's not there. It must be in the other hand. He asks you to guess again. You guess the other hand, but it's not there either. The paper has magically disappeared.

"Where did it go?" you wonder. The audience laughs. "What are they laughing at?"

Now you're really distracted. You try to focus on the magician's hands, but you're working overtime to figure out why the audience is laughing. "Are they laughing at me? What's happening?"

The trick continues. More toilet paper. More magic. The paper balls continue to disappear. You have no idea where they're going because you don't know the name of the trick. The audience doesn't either, but they have a unique perspective. They see the paper balls being thrown right over your head, seemingly right in front of your face.

The paper balls grow bigger and bigger. You become more and more amazed. The audience becomes more amazed too, but they aren't in awe of the paper disappearing. They're in awe of your awe and that you're so easily distracted.

People in the audience who watch all this take place think, "If that were me up there, there's no way I would fall for something so simple." And yet I have successfully performed this trick in front of a live audience more than two thousand times.

It does not matter the age of the person onstage or how educated the person is or the country I'm in. I have performed the trick for kids, teenagers, college students, and adults. I have performed the trick for doctors, lawyers, and seemingly every other vocation. One time I performed the trick for a guy who worked at NASA. I asked him after the show what he does at NASA. He said, and I quote, "I'm a systems analyst. It's my job to catch what other people miss."

It works every single time.

Performing this trick as part of my repertoire has taught me a valuable lesson. It shows that our focus and attention are so easily distracted. Misdirection is one of the most powerful tools at a magician's disposal. The secret to this trick is simply shifting the participant's focus to the point that they are too distracted to see what's right in front of them.

This trick is amazing to the person sitting onstage, until they stand up, walk back to their seat, and turn around to face the stage. Then they see the giant pile of toilet paper sitting on the floor behind where they had just been sitting. It's amazing what a shift in perspective can offer us.

I've spent almost my entire life studying the principles necessary to create an environment onstage in which people deceive themselves. It makes for great stage entertainment, but it's another story in our personal lives. Sadly, we are often so distracted by what others think of us that we miss the real magic.

When I began writing this book, it's as if the universe unleashed every distraction possible to seize my attention and keep me from the focus I needed to sit down and do the work. Has that ever happened to you? The question is, did those distractions come out of nowhere, or were they always there? They had always been there, of course. But now I had a new focus, and writing a book means taking a risk, so my mind did everything in its power to keep me focused on something else in order to keep me safe—safe from the potential failure of not finishing or the potential pain of negative reviews.

I not only had to keep my focus on the goal of finishing this book, I had to shift my focus away from the distractions. Sometimes I had to quiet the literal, physical noise distractions—like a TV in the next room—or find a different place to write entirely to distance myself from the interruptions of my kiddos. And none of this even begins to take into account the distractions of my phone—calls, text messages, push notifications, emails. "And since I'm already answering that text," I think, "I might as well go ahead and check Twitter and Instagram too."

What are the elements of your environments that limit your perspective, shifting your focus and contributing to stories that aren't true? It might be time to make some changes to the things in your environment that divert your attention away from what you should be most focused on. Don't set yourself up for failure by doing what I have often done, simply saying, "I just need to tune it out." Often you have the power not just to tune it out but to turn it off completely.

Find Mirrors You Can Trust

Leonardo da Vinci was once asked how he knew a work of art was complete. Think about that for a moment. If you were painting the *Mona Lisa*, how would you know when to step back, put down the paintbrush, and say, "That's it. It's complete."

According to da Vinci, he would walk away from the painting, eventually come back, and look at it in a mirror. Simply by changing his perspective, he could see things that weren't there before. I imagine he would then add a few strokes until it looked good in the mirror, then consider his work complete.

Do you know what would make my toilet paper trick truly impossible? Performing it in front of a mirror. That would offer the volunteer onstage a different perspective, limiting my ability to toss the paper balls right over their head. Mirrors can be powerful if we know how to use them.

We've been looking into mirrors for ages, trying to make sense of what we see. Even before we had mirrors, I'm quite certain human beings were curiously looking into reflective surfaces, sometimes peering deep into their own eyes, trying to figure out who they were. Most of the environments in our modern era are filled with mirrors.

"Mirror, mirror, on the wall, who's the fairest of them all?"

Mirrors have one job: to tell the truth about whatever is right in front of it, to tell the truth about the environment. Little do most people realize, a far more powerful mirror is already in the room each time I do the trick: the live audience. And it turns out, people make the best mirrors. But we have to make sure they're the right people. If the mirror is broken, it doesn't show an accurate reflection. Or worse, it could end up clouding your perspective.

What makes for the best mirror to tell the truth about our environment, or the story we're in? The right people. So the question is, what kind of mirrors are you allowing to speak into your life?

Perhaps one of the most important aspects of the environments you live and work in is the other voices in them. This includes the people you physically occupy those spaces with and the ones you interact with through the diet of information you regularly consume. Who are the mirrors in your environment? What stories do they tell you?

Sadly, for far too many, this becomes a difficult subject. Maybe you're reading this in your youth, feeling trapped at home in an environment you hate, purely because of the voices you're surrounded by. Maybe your life feels like a maze of broken mirrors, and every direction you turn, you feel forced to face another voice that crushes your wonder.

Others of us have more control over the mirrors in our environments than we often realize. It's time to exercise that control and create a seismic shift in your atmosphere. For some, that's as simple as clicking the unfollow button or picking up the remote control and changing the channel. If the feed of voices you have curated so far is not creating an atmosphere where wonder is sustainable, it's time to make some changes.

It is often said that you will be the same person five years from now that you are today except for two things: the books you read and the people you spend time with. Some leaders say you are the average of the five people you spend the most time with. While those statements feel a little oversimplified at times, I have experienced them to be true in my own life. The voices that speak into your life, whether they're authors, social media influencers, or news anchors, make a major contribution to the creation of your atmosphere. Add in the people you spend the most time with, and trying to be someone other than the sum total of who all those people are will be a constant uphill battle.

We're shaped by others because we are storytelling creatures, and the stories we're told all work to shape the stories we tell ourselves. Who are the other storytellers you're giving power to? They shape your perspective. Do they serve as an accurate mirror that helps you discover the truth of who you really are? Or do they misdirect your attention, leaving you cleverly deceived, and you're left to struggle with the lies you tell yourself? Surrounding yourself with the right people and removing the negative voices who are never constructive and only critical is essential.

I have learned many of these lessons the hard way. Some of the greatest contributors to the success I have experienced so far in my short life are the mentors and advisors I have surrounded myself with along the way. At times, I have wisely discerned the healthy mirrors from the unhealthy ones and been surrounded by voices of truth. Other times, I've not been so wise, and those have been some of the most difficult and challenging seasons of my life and career. Few things will create an atmosphere where wonder feels impossible to sustain faster than the wrong people.

One recent example is a business partner I took on in one of our companies. This person came into my world—stepped into my environment—on a mission to serve, with respect and admiration handed out in droves. I was lavished with praise and compliments daily. At the time, I was in a season of stress, buried in work and additional opportunities, and she was armed with the right set of strengths to fill the void I sensed in our team. But within a few short months, the compliments turned into constant criticism. No more "wow," just a constant source of unhealthy "how?" No wonder, just cynicism. I quickly learned what Bob Goff meant when he said, "Cynicism is fear posing as confidence."[2]

This person became a broken, unhealthy mirror that wreaked havoc on the culture I had worked so hard to create. Our environment went from being filled with joy and purpose to one of constant conflict. Gossip was spread among other members of our team. It was a toxic atmosphere and left me faced with a difficult decision.

What do you do in this scenario? You do what I have learned all great leaders do: protect your culture, so that you, along with those who are under your leadership, can work in an environment where wonder is sustained and toxicity doesn't crush your dreams, aspirations, and creativity. The paperwork, the client relationships, and all the other things that come along with ending a partnership were as messy as you might imagine. But once that season was behind us, the atmosphere I had fostered in the past slowly returned, and wonder was ready to do its magical work again.

Audit Your Environment

The good news is that once you're aware of your environment, you get to make some choices. You don't have to let broken mirrors define your reality. And you can find trusted mirrors to help remind you of the good story you're in.

It's time to do an audit. It's time to assess your atmosphere and ensure that it aligns with what your wonder is calling you toward. If the story your environment is telling—the sights, the sounds, and yes, even the smells—don't align with the story you want to live, it's time to make some changes. Some people complain about their "situation" but seem unwilling to make dramatic changes to their environment. If you want to turn on your wonder switch, and keep it on, staying in a toxic environment is not in service to pursuing a life of wonder and all that comes with it.

What good is it to experience magic that awakens your wonder but then allow it to be snuffed out by a harmful atmosphere? That's like going to the movies looking for a hit of wonder, only to return to a wonderless life. That's using the temporary magic as a medicator. Instead, search out and cultivate an atmosphere that serves as a motivator and keeps wonder alive.

What is warring against your wonder? What is conflicting with the story wonder is offering you? Is it your calendar? Your diet? Your "friends"? Your social media feed? The physical space you live or work in? It might be time to make some changes. Or it could just be time to go outside for a while. No, really—changing your environment might just mean spending more time in nature.

The Healing Power of Fresh Air

In her book *The Nature Fix*, author Florence Williams provides the research that confirms that spending time outdoors makes us happier, healthier, and yes, even more creative. And not only is going outside good for your health—not spending time outside carries negative consequences.

Research shows that nature boosts our immune system. If awe and wonder have similar effects on our physical health, and nature often awakens our wonder and leaves us in awe, it doesn't take long to connect the dots.

For example, your body is filled with something called natural killer cells—"NK cells" for short. They're white blood cells that send a message to virus-infected cells and tumors, telling them to "self-destruct." Studies show that spending time in nature increases the NK cell counts in our bodies.[3] And nature's effect on our NK cell count lasts long after we've come inside. How cool is that? In one study, even the smell of a forest reduced stress and lowered blood pressure because the phytoncides in cypress trees are antibacterial.[4]

There's much more research about how going outside positively affects our physical health, but perhaps the greatest impact is simply what being outdoors does for our mental and emotional well-being. Williams spent time in the desert with two psychologists, Dave Strayer and Paul Atchley, learning how a media-saturated environment greatly affects our ability to pay attention. Together they discuss how attention is a limited resource and that spending time in nature streamlines our choices. The result is a narrower focus, allowing us to be more present and tuned in to the world around us. We can maximize these effects by spending three full days in the great outdoors. Maybe it's time to pack a backpack and put on your hiking boots for a trek into the forest.

Maybe you're settling for the atmosphere you're in because it doesn't seem like there are any other options. Remember, things are not always as they seem. Sometimes you have to shift your perspective and turn around to look. Other times you have to close your eyes to see more clearly. What in your environment is distracting and diverting your attention away from where you could be looking? What is the story that all the sights, sounds, and smells around you are working together to tell?

The atmosphere you create at home matters. The atmosphere you create at work, whatever work looks like for you, matters. What would it look like to intentionally create a whole new atmosphere so that your wonder might be sustained?

Changing your environment, and the atmosphere in it, could change your life. Your wonderland awaits. And once you've created a new atmosphere and arrived at your wonderland, the imaginable will become tangible. And that's exactly the conversation we're due to have—when and how to put your wonder into action. Let's explore how to put your wonder to work.

CHAPTER 8

Wonder in Action

Moving from Complacency to Curiosity

On September 12, 1962, President John F. Kennedy stood in front of a crowd gathered at Rice Stadium in Houston, Texas, and said, "We choose to go to the moon."[1] Many consider this to be one of the most inspiring speeches ever delivered by a president. There is so much to learn from the speech as it relates to the story it told and how it shifted the stories Americans were telling themselves about what was possible. But why did Kennedy choose to go to the moon?

He answers that question in this historic speech, in short, by saying, "Because it is there." Take a look at this brief section from the transcript:

> But why, some say, the moon? Why choose this as our goal? And they may well ask why climb the highest mountain? Why, 35 years ago, fly the Atlantic? . . . We choose to go to the moon.

We choose to go to the moon in this decade and do the other things, not because they are easy, but because they are hard, because that goal will serve to organize and measure the best of our energies and skills, because that challenge is one that we are willing to accept, one we are unwilling to postpone, and one which we intend to win.

Kennedy finishes his speech by saying,

Many years ago the great British explorer George Mallory, who was to die on Mount Everest, was asked why did he want to climb it. He said, "Because it is there." Well, space is there, and we're going to climb it, and the moon and the planets are there, and new hopes for knowledge and peace are there. And, therefore, as we set sail we ask God's blessing on the most hazardous and dangerous and greatest adventure on which man has ever embarked.[2]

It *was* one of the most hazardous and dangerous and greatest adventures on which humanity has ever embarked. But we did it. On July 20, 1969, less than seven years after Kennedy proclaimed we would do so, astronaut Neil Armstrong stepped off his ladder and onto the surface of the moon and, with an estimated 650 million people watching in suspense, said those famous words, "That's one small step for a man. One giant leap for mankind."[3]

In recent years, the Apollo mission seems to have reentered the minds of Americans as a source of interest and recaptured our curiosity. Maybe this is because space travel seems to be entering a new season of possibility. Billionaires and entrepreneurs like Elon Musk, Jeff Bezos, and others are investing in establishing an entirely new industry in a landscape that only government agencies like NASA and its other subsidiaries, affiliates, and research facilities have previously occupied. But why are we so obsessed with exploring space? Is it merely, like President Kennedy said, because it's there?

As is often the case, there is probably more to the story. In her provocative podcast *Moonrise*, journalist Lillian Cunningham of the *Washington Post* reveals the chapters of the story that preceded Kennedy's aspirational call to put a man on the moon. As the official podcast description on iTunes states, "This is the real origin story behind America's decision to go to the moon. The story we learn starts with Sputnik, then President Kennedy's challenge, and ends with triumph: an American flag on the lunar surface. But in the 50 years that have passed since the moon landing, as presidential documents have been declassified and secret programs have been revealed, a wilder story has begun to emerge."[4]

Over the course of thirteen episodes, Cunningham brings to life the stories behind the story, connecting the dots of the nuclear arms race of the Cold War and even the birth of science fiction, ultimately revealing that the reason Kennedy chose to go to the moon was the same reason we all choose anything—because of the way the stories we're told stir our imagination, giving birth to curiosity that desires to answer the question, "What happens next?"

John F. Kennedy didn't want to go to the moon. At least not at first. All the transcripts and recorded conversations on the subject reveal Kennedy to be uninterested and at best pessimistic about America's place in the space race. But as Cunningham wonderfully brings into perspective through her work, the disaster Kennedy experienced through the botched Bay of Pigs invasion in Cuba left him needing a new narrative—something that would rally and inspire the American public, shifting the story of Kennedy's presidency.

Of the Cuban exiles who formed the brigade for the invasion at the Bay of Pigs, the majority—over 1,100—were taken prisoner. They remained in captivity for twenty months until finally their release was negotiated with Fidel Castro, and they returned to America in December 1962. Three months earlier, before they were even back on American soil, Kennedy had already taken the wonder of the American public that had been crushed by the fear and worries of the Cold War, reawakened it, and turned it into action by giving birth to curiosity. That curiosity would bring about a level of human achievement that the world had never seen.

What we find through our curiosity can help us reshape reality. As dreamers, innovators, and creative thinkers often prove, reality is sometimes merely an opinion. Years before Kennedy shifted our focus and flipped the wonder switch of America back on, science fiction writers were already telling stories about adventures of space travel. To some they seemed implausible, thus the reason for putting them in the category of "fiction." But these make-believe stories would later grant us permission to believe and make.

What can we learn from our ability to put a man on the moon? As one of humanity's greatest achievements, quite a bit. But there is also much to be learned by studying the curiosity that first led to the desire to go there in the first place—and the seemingly ludicrous belief that it might be possible.

Wonder in Action

Do you have a memory of staring up into space as a kid? I have a specific memory of my grandfather coming into the bedroom

I slept in when I spent the night at my grandparents' house. He whispered into my ear, "The stars are falling." With my curiosity piqued, I pulled myself out of my sleepy dreams, and he pulled me out of bed and carried me outside.

There was a hill in my grandparents' backyard. We would lie there on our backs staring up at the night sky, confirming that the newscast the night before had correctly predicted the soon-coming meteor shower. Indeed, the stars were falling, and it was so freaking cool.

Unfortunately, far too few of us look up at the stars anymore because other shiny things have captured our curiosity. The flickering pixels of screens. Even the social media influencers we consider to be the stars of today and tomorrow. We're more curious about what happens in the stories of those we aspire to be like than we are about what happens in our own. What might be possible if we allow our curiosity to drive our own story and ability to shine?

Just like we discovered about the power of human imagination in chapter 5, when you flip the wonder switch back on, everything about your curiosity gets flipped too.

Early in this book we looked at some aspects of wonder and discovered that wonder isn't just a feeling; it's a state. I hope you're beginning to understand that it's almost a way of living—an openness to the magic that is all around you and all it offers you. To be awake to wonder, to have your wonder switch on, is to live with an awareness of that magic and a willingness to allow it to do its transformative work when you encounter it.

But what does that transformation give birth to? It gives birth to curiosity. Curiosity, as my friend Amber Rae once told me during a podcast interview, is wonder in action.

The definitions of wonder that we've explored up to this point have been in the form of nouns. But regardless of which dictionary you open, *wonder* is also a verb. When we move from wonder as a noun to wonder as a verb, we move from being to doing. We move from a mere state of astonishment to a practiced *lifestyle* of curiosity. And curiosity beckons us. It's what turns the whisper of wonder into a bold call—a demand even—that says, "Satisfy me, or I will drive you insane." But can curiosity ultimately be satisfied?

We've explored the fact that wonder is linked to meaning and purpose in your life by pointing to the "why" that helps you find your "way" and that it can even decrease your worry and anxiety by changing how you use your imagination. Genuine curiosity is when wonder carries skeptics from the feel-good land of woo-woo and into the real world of creativity and innovation in both their life and work, because curiosity cultivates creativity. It is the primary driver of successful problem-solving, making it one of the most transformative aspects of wonder. It will carry you from dreaming to doing.

Whether you consider yourself a dreamer or not, innovation is something that should matter to us all. *Innovation* isn't just a business term. It isn't something that matters only if you want to build a rocket ship that can land on the moon. For example, many people believe going to the moon didn't really matter outside of proving that it could be done. Yet the Apollo mission still impacts our day-to-day lives in ways we often don't realize, and in ways I never would have guessed or imagined.

The technology NASA developed in order to land on the moon led to the innovation of heart monitors, pacemakers, dialysis treatment, fire-resistant clothing, cordless power tools, the Dustbuster, and much more. Even the shoes on your feet and the alarm system that protects your house are based on discoveries made during the Apollo mission.[5] Innovation changed everything and has improved our lives in countless ways.

So what would it look like for you to be innovative at work? That might be an obvious question and, in some ways, easy to answer. But what would it look like to become more innovative at home or in the way you lead your family? What would personal innovation look like to you? Don't settle for the status quo, doing things a certain way because that's the way they've always been done. What if there's a new you waiting to be discovered? What if the story you're living could change? What if . . . ?

Innovation is for more than just "big business." Successful organizations of all kinds and sizes, from tech companies to nonprofits, innovate every day to create and shape the future. But innovation isn't a natural talent doled out to a select few. Whether you're a leader of a Fortune 500 company, a stay-at-home mom or dad, or anything in between, approaching your life in innovative ways by developing your curiosity will help you solve many of the problems you face throughout your day, regardless of what those problems entail.

What does this mean for you? Often we're told that the solution is to try harder. And your personal innovation as a leader (something I consider every human being to be) may indeed include trying harder at some things. But sometimes when we think we lack focus, discipline, and drive, what we actually lack most is curiosity. People look for "plug and play" solutions. Wonder isn't like that. And because curiosity is wonder in action, the reawakening of wonder is where creativity and innovation thrive. Let's explore why.

Curiosity Breeds Creativity

Creativity is simply your brain's response to the problems you discover. We solve problems every day in our minds. And yet many believe "I'm not creative."

As I mentioned, I hear this lie frequently. Of course, when they tell me this, no one is intentionally lying to me to pull the wool over my eyes. It is genuinely how they feel. As we've discovered, our feelings often lie to us because we craft narratives that protect us and keep us safe.

If we, as the characters in our own stories, are decidedly "not creative," then an endless list of easy excuses permits us not to create and innovate in our lives and work. And of course then we also don't take risks, because failure is always a possibility. So we play it safe and choose not to engage in creative acts, lest we potentially fail. The narrative of success we adopt as true by never taking risks ends up breeding complacency.

Let's be clear, again: everyone is creative. Regardless of how you use your imagination, you indeed use it to create stories of possibility. Some of them just don't end well. But let's shift our focus to positive and productive creativity in the form of innovative problem-solving. Is that something you are naturally capable of doing? Is that a talent you have?

It's not a talent Einstein had. He said, "I have no special talents. I am only passionately curious."[6] Yet his self-admitted lack of talent didn't keep him from what is easily considered creative genius. What about the world's most renowned creative artists? Is their creativity baked in, meaning they're gifted from above with natural creative talent?

If we go back to the Renaissance, we discover a time that wasn't so unlike our own. It was a time of discovery and innovation at what must have felt like a rapid pace. It was also a season in which artists created some of the world's most revered masterpieces. Leonardo da Vinci, who was known for painting and sculpting, also became known for his ability as an engineer. His creative vision permitted him to draw things like "flying machines," which he even built and tested, though unsuccessfully, back in 1496.

Surely da Vinci, with his wide array of talents bridging both art and science and with such an imaginative body of work, had to be naturally creative, right? Yet according to his own words in some of his journals and writings, even da Vinci credits his creativity to a cultivated sense of curiosity:

> I roamed the countryside searching for answers to things I did not understand. Why shells existed on the tops of mountains along with the imprints of coral and plants and seaweed usually found in the sea. Why the thunder lasts a longer time than that which causes it, and why immediately on its creation the lightning becomes visible to the eye while thunder requires time to travel. How the various circles of water form around the spot which has been struck by a stone, and why a bird sustains itself in the jar. These questions and other strange phenomena engage my thought throughout my life.[7]

Da Vinci's notebooks don't just reveal words; they reveal initial sketches of some of our modern era's most transformative inventions, including not only a flying machine in the form of an airplane but also a helicopter, a submarine, and even a car. How did da Vinci imagine these things? Through observation. Through "searching for answers to things I did not understand." By asking, "Why?"

Five hundred years later, Neil Armstrong flew on a flying machine all the way to the moon and landed on it, later echoing da Vinci by saying, "Mystery creates wonder and wonder is the basis of man's desire to understand."[8]

Curiosity, our wonder in action, pushes us forward to search and explore and end up in places we never could have previously imagined. You don't need any special genes or inherent talents or superpowers other than what you were already born with—a child-like wonder that gives birth to curiosity and helps you imagine things you don't currently see with your own eyes.

Counterfeit Curiosity

When was the last time you paid attention and truly observed something around you? Really paid attention to the magic? Remember, it exists even in the seemingly mundane. When you allow curiosity to follow the bread crumbs of magic, it will take you to places you didn't expect. You may even discover answers to questions you weren't even asking. And that, perhaps, is one of the most valuable lessons I've learned about curiosity. In a world where we have information at our fingertips, counterfeit curiosity thrives.

The way people respond to magic tricks in a year like 2020, the year I'm writing this book, has revealed a counterfeit form of curiosity. It involves a line of questioning that poses as curiosity and gets justified as such but doesn't lead to the kind of creativity and innovation that genuine curiosity leads to. Genuine curiosity takes a humbler approach by being open to being surprised.

Creativity is simply your brain's response to the problems you discover. We all, regardless of vocation, have problems to solve. Whether the problem is simply, "We're stuck, and we are capable of coming up with creative solutions to this problem," or "I need joy, and filling this blank canvas will solve for it."

Research shows that the brain chemicals that are present

during and associated with creativity and innovation are linked to a kind of curiosity that is less focused on answers and more focused on exploration. It's as if there's a difference between "I need to know how this works, so just tell me the answer" and "I'm intrigued and am willing to venture into the mysterious unknown, curious about what I might learn or find along the way."

Performing magic tricks has taught me that people immediately want to know how something works. Over the last year, it's been interesting to give keynotes alongside the performance of a few magic tricks. When I give a talk on the value of wonder and curiosity, people justify their desire for me to tell them the secret with the value I placed on curiosity. I'll say, "Sorry, I can't tell you the secret. Sit in the wonder and just say wow, not how." And then they'll respond with, "But you just told us how healthy it is to be curious, and I'm curious how you did that."

Counterfeit curiosity demands answers, answers we desire for no other reason than to release the tension we feel from not knowing. That's a new tension that generations before us didn't struggle with as much because Wikipedia didn't exist. The information age, combined with the technology to access that information at our fingertips, has created within us a sort of comfort in the ability to find answers. But genuine curiosity embraces mystery, explores the unknown, and is comfortable doing so regardless of the outcome because the goal isn't so predefined as, say, an answer to a specific question.

We often set out with the goal of satisfying our curiosity, but I'm not sure that the goal of genuine curiosity is to "be satisfied." I think we're wired to be curious because it's how we create and grow as human beings. Real, productive, helpful curiosity that is rooted in wonder is more like jazz. Jazz is curious.

Famous jazz artist Louis Armstrong once advised, "Never play a thing the same way twice."[9] Maybe that was his opinion based on his experience, but it turns out, there's new scientific research that suggests this idea is world-class advice. No surprise, coming from a legend in his field.

Jazz is certainly not the only genre of music that can lead to composing new works on the spot, but improvisation is jazz's defining characteristic. And this willingness to venture into uncharted territory, not knowing the outcome, is teaching us a lot about embracing exploration and the magic that can be discovered along the way. A new study by scientists at Johns Hopkins discovered that when jazz musicians improvise, the parts of their brains that are linked to self-censoring and inhibition, like the prefrontal cortex, quite literally turn off.[10]

What does this teach us about the power of curiosity?

First, it begins to help us understand that when we engage in acts of genuine curiosity, we are permitted to explore with less fear of failing. In a cool way, curiosity becomes greater than fear, decreasing our need to self-censor and inhibit our creativity, and instead permits self-expression and increases creative flow.

Second, it teaches us that genuine curiosity is more related to a willingness to explore and improvise and is less about merely finding answers to questions just for the sake of knowing.

This certainly lines up with my experience as a professional magician, offering insight into the twenty years of that nonstop line of questioning that all magicians face from members of our audiences: "How did you do that?" Is the asking of that question an act of genuine curiosity? Or is it simply an attempt to avoid the discomfort our information age–trained brains feel in response to mystery?

I believe it's the latter. You may feel the urge to know how a trick works for the sake of not being "driven crazy" by not knowing the answer. But does that intense desire to understand serve you all that well? Would you not be better served by leaning into the mystery and allowing your curiosity to take you on a journey into the unknown?

Of course, there is a time to ask, "How did you do that?" "How?" is a powerful question. But we must reclaim our ability to say "Wow!" without immediately jumping to "How?"

Wow before How

I've found that most people's minds tend to gravitate in one direction or the other—"wow" or "how"—but we can all get better at both.

I think of myself as a "wow" person. My wife, Kate, is a "how" person. Both come with their temptations and potential traps that can limit our thinking and perspective. Without my wife, I'd probably be bankrupt. Again. I'm not joking that it's probable I would be sleeping on a street somewhere. But you'd better believe I'd also be on the street corner by day, with a deck of cards in my hand, ready to stir the imaginations of passersby and pass my hat in an effort to get back on my feet.

The reality is, as a wow person, I tend to be blind to the how part of the plan. Kate, along with members of my team, has learned the proper way to meet my wow ideas with questions of how, for the sake of practicing wisdom, making plans, and being responsible. But we've built a culture of curiosity that allows us to wow and how at the appropriate times and in the proper ways.

It hasn't always been this way. Early on in our marriage, there were times when an idea would come to me. I could be anywhere.

In the shower, or driving down the road in the car. These are places where ideas seem to "hit me."

This is how it used to happen.

A glorious idea would fall out of the sky and into my brain. My most immediate thought was usually, "This is genius!" Was it actually genius? No, not usually. But it sure seemed that way at first. Naturally, when these ideas popped up, they begged to be shared. And because Kate is often in closest proximity, she was usually the first to hear the idea.

"Okay, babe . . . I have a genius idea! Are you ready for this?"

"Oh boy. What is it?" she would say, usually without even shifting her focus from the task at hand.

"Okay, what if . . ." And then I would share the idea, with the enthusiasm of P. T. Barnum outside a circus tent, beckoning people to step right up and experience the magic in all its glory. And what would she say?

"Wow! You are a creative genius! I am reminded over and over again, each and every time I hear your ideas, of why I married you!"

Right? No, of course not. She's a how person. "How" people never respond that way. At least not without intentionally building a culture of curiosity.

Before she would say anything, she'd usually raise her eyebrows, squint her eyes a bit, and depending on where we were, even place a hand on a hip. Then it happened. The word. "How?"

Don't get me wrong, there were often a lot more words. But that was usually the first one. "How in the world are you going to do that?" "How is that going to work?" "How would that even be possible?"

When an idea is met with "How?" too soon, it stops wonder in its tracks. The switch gets turned off, and creativity and innovation come to a screeching halt.

Has that ever happened to you? Do you have a memory of being so excited to share an idea with someone, whether someone on your team or a family member, and instead of hearing, "Wow, that sounds amazing!" the way you had anticipated, your idea was met with hows and questions of its validity and a long list of explanations as to why your idea would never work?

A lot of great ideas never see the light of day because they are how'd to death—wow never has a chance to breathe. They have so much potential, but their development depends on their being met with "Wow!" well before "How?"

Magicians have a unique creative process. One of the pillars of that process is that we don't think "outside the box" because to us, there is no box to begin with. We create without constraints, not because some constraints will not eventually be introduced but because the art of illusion makes just about anything possible. We begin with what we want to create, then find a way later. In other words, we start with a wow, then figure out how.

Great leaders, great creators, great parents, great partners—all great human beings have to learn to do the same. There is a right time to say wow, and a time to ask how. We need to learn the right response at the proper time. Now, fifteen years of marriage later, Kate has learned how to help keep me dreaming, and I've learned, thanks mostly to her, the value of a plan.

We can't build a plan without spending time with how people, getting answers to questions about how something will work. "How" people have the extraordinary ability to peer into the future and see all the potential problems, which is a valuable superpower when leveraged appropriately and at the proper time in the creative, innovative process. To succeed, we need both wow and how.

I believe the trick to balancing both is to allow the wow part of the process to breathe, without rushing on to how too quickly. This often comes down to awareness. Specifically, the awareness of the words we use and the awareness of which step of the creative process we're in. Remember, wow before how.

For most people, the moment I describe the differences between wow people and how people, it's immediately clear which one they are. Understanding which type you are helps you lean into your natural strengths and best leverage your superpower. But just in case you don't know which type you are, your words serve as a clue to which role you're playing and where in the process you find yourself.

"How" language is often focused on finding reasons for why something won't work. Again, there is certainly a time for this language, and it can be helpful if used for the right reasons, at the right time. But far too often "how" language is simply used to react to the natural threat we feel in response to wonder and curiosity. You will hear others or even catch yourself using language like the following:

"I don't know if . . ."
"But the rules we need to follow are . . ."
"I'm not sure if we should be questioning . . ."
"That's not how that works . . ."
"That's not very practical . . ."
"That has never been done before . . ."
"It didn't work for them . . ."
"That's going to be too much work . . ."
"We can't afford to . . ."
"Yes, but . . ."

Do you notice a common theme throughout those phrases? There's a consistent focus on reasons why something isn't possible.

Because wonder feels disruptive and threatening to the status quo, our brains kick into overdrive to find an excuse to play things safe. It's easier to get back in line and go about business as usual than it is to cause a ruckus.

"I don't know if . . ." is valid. Of course we don't know everything about what we're setting out to do, but that should never keep us from trying. We didn't know how to go to the moon. But we decided to go because we looked up and said, "Wow! What if we could go there?" And then we figured it out along the way. The rule book was thrown out the window. We had to question authority. It was far from practical. No one had done it before, let alone had the audacity to say it could be done.

Could you imagine if NASA's leadership would have told Kennedy, "Sorry, but that's going to be too much work."

What if they had said, "We can't afford to go to the moon." Yet Kennedy's administration found a way, and so did Johnson when he picked up the mantle.

If you find yourself naturally bent toward using this kind of language, it's probably more helpful to work on *reframing* your how-driven questions than to try to change how you're naturally wired. Pause and ask yourself, "How can I be creative rather than destructive?" Often this simply requires shifting your how questions to more open-ended wow language. These comments and questions are less final in nature and more open to possibility.

Instead of responding to ideas with a declaration such as "That won't work because . . . ," simply ask something like, "Is it possible that _____ could happen?" That leads the idea sharer to pause in consideration and think, "Yes, I suppose it's possible that could happen." And then their brainstorming and creative problem-solving have permission to carry on and keep exploring possibilities.

Other examples include, "Can you imagine what you would do when _____ happens?" and one of my personal favorites, "What if . . . ?" As we've discovered, "What if?" is a powerful question because while it can spur our imagination to worry about the negative potential outcomes, it also opens us up to positive possibilities.

Paying attention to this kind of language can clue you in on when your response to wonder is overtaking your curiosity and crushing your ability to think in innovative ways. Once you develop an awareness of this language, the next step is to become aware of whether you're saying wow and how at the appropriate times. Just as in the execution of a sleight-of-hand magic trick, this timing is critical.

To create and innovate from a place of wonder, we must learn to let wow have its day.

I often recommend to leaders to separate team meetings into wow meetings and how meetings. If you have undisciplined how people on your team who are great at poking holes in every idea, it's sometimes best to exclude them from the initial brainstorming process. We have to create safe spaces where unrestricted, creative brainstorming can occur in an environment where anything is possible.

The wow before how concept doesn't apply only to the workplace. It works at home too. It is relevant to the way we interact with our partners and friends and especially to the way we raise our children. If you're naturally a how person, the next time a coworker swings into your office or inbox with a big, audacious goal, remember to let wow breathe. When your ten-year-old daughter informs you she wants to be the first female president, let wow breathe. Please don't allow the wonder that was once crushed in you to crush the wonder of those around you. The next time you hear someone share a dream or even just an idea, find the wow, say it out loud, and let wonder breathe. There will be plenty of time to ask how later.

If you're naturally a wow person, you have to develop close relationships with people who need clear plans and road maps before they buy into an idea. Please understand that their need to do so does not disqualify your idea. There is much to learn from those who like plans. If you tend to think, "I don't know how this could fail," then you need the presence of a how person in your life, or things aren't going to go well for you. It might feel like they're raining on your parade, but try to learn to keep your wonder switch turned on and continue to see possibility where others see only risk. We all need each other, and we can accomplish far more together than we ever could on our own. Together, we can shoot for the moon.

Your Moon Shot

Maybe you want to start that business you've always dreamed of. Maybe you want to step outside your comfort zone to cultivate a relationship you've been desiring. Maybe it's time to ask for a raise or promotion at work, to better position you to live the purpose you feel you're on this planet to fulfill. What is your moon shot? What do you aspire to accomplish or become?

I hope your curiosity is beginning to become greater than your fear of the unknown. If not, what can you do to fuel it? How can you put your wonder to work as your wonder switch begins to turn back on? How can you be more intentional about observing the world around you? What is the last experience you had that made you think, "Wow!"

Up until this point, I've given the information age a pretty hard time, but it does come with a long list of benefits. As with most things, it's really about finding balance. Awe-inspiring images and stories that can awaken our wonder are merely a click away. When is the last time you allowed your curiosity to take you on a trip down the rabbit hole to wonderland?

Eleanor Roosevelt once said, "I could not, at any age, be content to take my place by the fireside and simply look on. Life was meant to be lived. Curiosity must be kept alive. One must never, for whatever reason, turn his back on life."[11] Perhaps it was the value she placed on curiosity that led Mrs. Roosevelt also to say, "I think, at a child's birth, if a mother could ask a fairy godmother to endow it with the most useful gift, that gift would be curiosity."

If we continue to turn back to the mindset we had as children, we find how much easier it was to live curious lives back then. No one taught us as children how to be curious. We just were. No one asks how to motivate babies to observe the world around them. We naturally explored our surroundings. Curiosity doesn't die, any more than wonder dies. It's crushed and lulled asleep, and takes our ability to be curious into a coma along with it.

Have you turned your back on life? Did someone take the wow of your youth and how it to death, stealing your most useful gift? If so, it's not too late. Through a reawakening of wonder, your curiosity can come back to life. But once it does, you must cultivate an environment where that "wonder in action" can thrive and be sustained. Sir Ken Robinson said, "You can't just give someone a creativity injection. You have to create an environment for curiosity and a way to encourage people and get the best out of them."[12] Curiosity can propel your rocket to the moon, but unless it's sustainable, you'll run out of fuel.

Taking a moon shot requires the right attitude and the right atmosphere. You have to develop a Wonder Mindset and the ability to sustain that mindset through the right environment. The combination of those two things will make you unstoppable, taking you to places you never thought possible.

CHAPTER 9

Right Your Story

The Key to a Life Filled with Magic

Throughout this book, we've explored the myriad ways that you've been led to tell yourself stories that aren't true and how all those stories have formed a narrative that drives your belief system and therefore your habits and behavior. Once you begin to understand that, it becomes easier to see that just about every problem is a storytelling problem.

Along the way, we've also explored the role that wonder plays in permitting you to embrace a new narrative and a new mindset and to create new atmospheres in your environment, all enabling you to step into ownership of a new story.

I like to think of this process as "story righting." To guide you through the story-righting process, I'm going to walk you through the five steps we've utilized in our group coaching and Mastermind programs to move others from awakening their wonder to attaining the creative, magical lives they were meant to live.

Before we begin, it's important to know one thing. The goal of righting your story doesn't mean the story you've lived up until this point has been the wrong one. It's just incomplete.

At the beginning of this book, I introduced the Transformation Map and the idea that all change is driven by going from an old story to a new one. When you look at the map now with a fresh perspective, where do you find yourself?

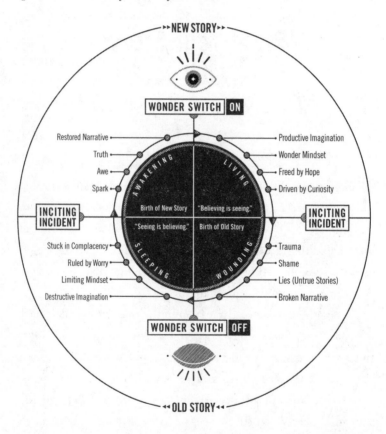

Remember, as discussed in chapter 1, we adopt a variety of narratives throughout our lives, and you might find yourself in a different place in the circle of transformation in one narrative compared to another. By understanding the role that inciting incidents play in our stories, you can begin to see how trauma can lead to a broken narrative, which means it's possible to have a part of your life driven by a narrative absent of trauma, and therefore less impacted by it.

In more simple terms, it could be similar to a fear of flying on airplanes because of a close call while on a flight, or closely witnessing the events of 9/11, and instead, experiencing no anxiety while driving a car on a highway. It doesn't matter if planes are statistically safer than cars. The trauma you experienced of 9/11 affected the narrative you've formed around flying, but the narrative you've formed around driving cars is less affected due to a lack of trauma. If you've been involved in a traumatic car crash, that's a different story—literally.

Every facet of the story you've lived so far has played a role in shaping who you are today. But if you've lost your sense of wonder and settled for a counterfeit version of the life you were meant to live, it's time for some course correction. You need to get your story back on track, and this simple five-step process will transform your life by helping you make the leap from a broken narrative filled with untrue stories to a new story of meaning, purpose, and possibility. Now, just because this process is simple, that does not mean it's easy. It is simple to understand but difficult to execute. The path toward healing can be challenging, but it's a path I have walked, and continue to walk, and I promise the work is worth it. A new story awaits.

Step 1: Awaken

If you've read all eight chapters up until this point, this first step shouldn't surprise you. Naturally, the first step in your story of transformation is to wake up. Awaken from the slumber. Awaken your wonder. Everything in this book has had the goal of leading you to this place—where you refuse to go back to business as usual. Where you find the courage to stop settling. Where you resolve never to go back to coasting and complacency and therefore miss all the magic. You were meant for more, and now that you are awake to it, lean in. Be fully present, and pay attention to the magic that can spark your wonder.

As you pay attention right now, what are you feeling? Be mindful of whatever it is. Is it pain? Suffering? What story are you giving that suffering? Is that story true? Do you feel worry? Anxiety? Fear? Is it healthy fear that serves you well and tells you something valuable? Or is the dark side of your imagination at work, leading you to worry for no good reason?

If it's helpful (and it probably is), write down how you're feeling—your pain, fears, delights. Assess where they're coming from. Grab a blank sheet of paper or open a journal, and grab a pen and write it down. Develop a regular practice of walking through this process. Imagine you are developing a character for a story. When screenwriters go through this process, even if the details don't make the final script, it's best to write from a deep understanding of the lead character in the story. How has the story you've lived thus far shaped and developed your character? Start with what you know.

Keep in mind that this is not a onetime step. This is a process that gets revisited regularly. For some, it's monthly. For others it could even be daily. Flipping your wonder switch may come with a major awakening that serves as a defining moment in your life, but we continue to wake up to more and more as we become more fully present and aware. The reality of the wonder switch is that it's a dimmer switch. You can turn it on or off, but it can also fade up and down.

It is from this place of being fully awake and aware that you begin to see in ways that you never could before, permitting you to reimagine what you aspire to do and be. Many people attempt to work toward a goal, only to get stuck. It's often because they skipped this first step of awakening.

Step 2: Aspire

What are your goals and aspirations? What are your dreams? For many, these questions are difficult to answer. Much of this has to do with the wonder switch and whether it's in the on or off position. We tend to aspire toward only the things we believe are possible. Believing is seeing, and sometimes it's hard to see beyond the situations we currently find ourselves in. The more your wonder stirs your imagination in new and exciting ways, and the more you develop your Wonder Mindset, the easier this step of the process will become.

I meet people every week in my work who have either dreams they've given up on or dreams they've never had enough wonder or courage to pursue because of the ways their wonder has been wounded in their past. I've talked with people who have a dream to write a book, make a film, learn photography, or learn to paint. Some have personal financial goals that feel hopeless, like get out of debt or make enough extra money to start a family, send a kid to college, pay for a wedding, or take that trip they've dreamed of taking their entire lives. Many have dreams that are far simpler but, due to broken narratives, still feel out of reach. They'd like to find the courage to get on an airplane for the first time to go on their first vacation or visit a loved one in another state. Others dream of finding the courage to share their feelings with someone they've loved for a long time or to pursue a perfect position at work they've always felt more suited for.

Maybe you don't relate to any of these kinds of dreams. Maybe you still find it hard to dream at all. If so, that's okay. Give yourself some time. The more you revisit this framework and continue to right the stories you're telling and living, the more wins you'll experience, which will only permit you to keep dreaming bigger. So much of this book emphasizes that more is possible than you currently realize, but there's nothing wrong with dreaming small at first. I've been guilty of being impatient with those who dream too small, but have grown over time to understand that sometimes you have to climb the first mountain in order to see the next one.

If we tap into this exercise as a professional storyteller might when writing a screenplay, this is the part of the process where we think about the story with the end in mind. What is this character setting out to accomplish? What does she want to attain by the end of the movie? What journey is she going on? This is not the time to worry about the conflict she'll experience along the way, and all the potential pain and suffering that come with it. There will be plenty of time to deal with that later. Start with the end in mind and proceed without being attached to it.

As you focus on your dreams and aspirations, write them down. Writing them down makes them real. As you do, pay attention to your language. For example, instead of writing, "I want to run a marathon," write, "I'm training to run a marathon next year." If what you want to attain is financial freedom by being debt free and saving up for an emergency fund, instead of saying, "If we can get out of debt, then . . .," say, "When we get out of debt . . ." Not if, but when. This exercise gets stronger the more you complete the story. If you allow yourself to create an aspirational image of what the final scene of the marathon story looks like, it probably includes the finish line, the celebration, the toast, the speech, and the hugs from family and friends. Develop that vision.

Changing your language to match that image is your ticket to jump-starting the rewiring of your brain. Allow your Wonder Mindset to establish those new neural pathways by changing the language you use and the story you tell yourself in the process. The more intentional you are, the more effective this practice will be.

For example, if you want to attain a weight-loss goal, instead of writing, "I want to lose weight," write, "I am taking control of my personal health by saying goodbye to ten pounds in the next six months." The first is generic. The other is specific and measurable. One contains words like *want* and *lose*. I don't know about you, but when I lose something, that means I go searching for it because I need to find it. I don't want to "lose" pounds; otherwise my subconscious might go searching for what I lost, without my being fully aware of it. I'm not losing those pounds. I'm letting them go, with no desire to see them ever again.

Can you see how our stories sometimes need correcting?

Having specific, measurable goals and writing them down brings our aspirations out of the clouds and makes them real. Let your wonder lead the way. As you do, you're going to dream bigger, as if anything is possible. This is a time for wow.

This is not the step of the process where you constantly pause and ask, "How?" or you'll how your aspirations to death. Are you seeing opportunities or only the obstacles? If you find yourself distracted by all the potential reasons you're going to fail, you're still falling prey to the temptation of how, and now is not the time.

Go ahead. Let your imagination run wild. What do you aspire to do and become?

Step 3: Align

Now you've spent time letting wonder have its way. You've explored the possibilities and written down a goal you aspire to accomplish. What's next? This is where the real work of story righting begins. It's time to align the story you're telling yourself with the story you want to live.

Look at the aspirations you just wrote down. If you made a whole list, great! Focus on one of them for a moment. Read your aspiration. Read it out loud if you're willing and able.

Now here's the magic question: What would you need to believe to be true about yourself to achieve that goal?

If what you need to believe doesn't align with what you currently believe, it's time to do some work. In other words, if the story you want to live doesn't align with the story you're currently telling yourself about who you are and what you're capable of, there's some story righting to do.

Forming new habits, developing your mindset, and making any necessary shifts in atmosphere are all tools at your disposal for righting your story. This is the heart of the story-righting process. It leads you to experience the magic of what psychologists call cognitive dissonance.

Here are some helpful questions as you seek to align your story:

What is your focus right now? Are you distracted? Has something misdirected your attention?

Are you focused on what you don't want? Or tuned in to what you want?

What wounded your wonder in the past that needs to be explored and healed?

How is what happened in your past showing up in the present?

Have you lost your "why"? If so, has losing that why caused you to lose your way?

Most importantly: What are the changes you need to make to get back to your why?

In professional storytelling, this is the stage where you discover the connection between the internal problems of a character's life and the external problems they experience in the world around them. The overwhelming majority of clients who come to us with an external problem come to realize in time that the problem they're facing is actually an internal problem. I sometimes make excuses for my actions that I incorrectly assume are outside my control, without realizing that I have designed a life that aligns with my narrative, whether it is true or not. My behavior is driven by my brain's attempt to validate that a story is true.

You may realize you're headed in a direction you never planned on. That's okay. The first step in going somewhere new is deciding that you don't want to stay where you are.

Each of the first three steps of this framework is designed to help guide you in your search for clarity. Clarity is what all great storytellers are constantly in search of. Once we have clarity, we can continue the process of creating. Until then, it's easy to feel stuck, unsure of what happens next. And remember, all great stories ask the question, "What happens next?"

Step 4: Accountability

We are social beings, designed to live life in connection with one another. Once you've gained clarity about the changes you need to make and begun to take action by aligning the old story and the new story, it's time to be held accountable for the commitments you've made to yourself.

Now it's important to assess your relationships. Who are the key people in your life? Where does your sense of love and belonging come from? Stories aren't meant to be lived alone, and righting your story alone is challenging, if not impossible. We are hurt in relationships, but we are healed in relationships as well.

Can you imagine Luke Skywalker trying to save the galaxy all on his own? And how engaging the Star Wars saga would have been without the entire cast of characters? Han Solo, Chewbacca, R2-D2, C-3PO—they aren't there just for comedic relief. Luke needed them for the journey. They championed him, but they also held him accountable. And even during the times they were nowhere to be found, Luke had Yoda to guide him back to a place of being fully awake and aware. Yoda reminded Luke of who he was and what he aspired to accomplish and become along the way.

Being in relationship with others will become a primary source of strength for your journey. It is astounding how many of our Mastermind group participants come into our program after being stuck for years, only to go on to accomplish their goals quickly, sometimes in only a few months' time. This is a direct result of gaining clarity around their story—by asking what happens next, doing the difficult work of healing and alignment, and being accountable to a small group of like-minded friends.

Who is your cast of characters? Whom are you going to invite to journey along with you? Who will hold you accountable to the commitments you've made to right your story? Who are the mirrors you trust to reflect your story back to you accurately? Choose wisely, and you'll go on to accomplish more together than you ever would have accomplished on your own.

Step 5: Attain

Finally, the part we've all been waiting for. You've cultivated a life that has allowed your wonder to awaken. You're fully alive, present, and tuned in. You've developed a vision of what you aspire to accomplish and become. You've aligned the story you want to live with the story you're telling yourself. You've built a small team of supporters and submitted to the accountability of the group. There's just one step remaining in your story-righting journey: do the work.

It's time to take action and attain your goals. It's time to push through the conflict that will always find a way to creep into your story. Practice gratitude for it as you experience it, because everything you do prepares you for everything you will do. The challenges will come. They always do. But with each and every chapter, you will attain not only goals but also wisdom, meaning, joy, and more.

We often believe that the huge problems we face as our stories unfold will always need a huge solution. That's a myth—one of the tricks we fall for. We solve big problems with small actions, one step at a time. A tiny pebble in your shoe feels like a huge deal. But once you remove it, you realize how little effort it took to have a huge impact on your life. It takes only a tiny pebble to have a ripple effect. Small steps, healthy habits, and repeated actions with the right attitude and mindset along the way eventually turn into attaining the future you've dreamed of. You will have realized your power and successfully taken agency of your story.

Right your story.

The Space Between

As you allow your wonder to help you make the leap from an old story to the new one, there will eventually come a time when you get stuck in the in-between—the space between "no longer" and "not yet." Don't be discouraged. This is called "liminal space," and while it can be messy, it is also beautiful. There is magic in the in-between.

I first discovered the concept of liminal space while talking with my friend John Bucher. Driving down an interstate late at night, I was venting about the season of life I was in. I had stepped out of an old story, putting a season of life behind me, and was ready to move on to the next chapter. Obviously, I did this with the intention of stepping into a new story—a new season based on a new vision of what could be. Flipping on my wonder switch had given birth to some new possibilities, and I was ready to make them a reality.

But they hadn't become a reality. Not yet. It felt like, potentially, not ever. I felt stuck. After explaining my situation to John with a tone of impatience and frustration, he chuckled in his usual jolly way, and with the joyful tone that consistently oozes out of him, he said, "Ah, Harris. It's all good, man. You're just in liminal space, that's all. I'm so excited for you."

"I'm sorry, what kind of space?" I had never heard of this concept before. As he described liminality from multiple perspectives—from architecture to spiritual formation—I began to grasp why I felt so uncomfortable. When you're between the old story and the new story, you feel like there's no story. When you don't know what story you find yourself in, you feel like you're floating through space, grasping for anything that might anchor you back in a reality that offers clarity.

The reason John was so excited for me, and why I have now grown to appreciate the space between, is because this space is where we grow. It's our becoming. As is commonly said, it's about the journey, not the destination.

The moment our wonder is awakened, we begin to see differently. Our wonder takes us to new heights and kick-starts new journeys, but those journeys aren't necessarily completed overnight. Along the way, you're going to get stuck from time to time, simply because your next step will not be clear. One of the most beautiful offerings of wonder is its unique ability to allow you to lean into the mystery. Embrace the magic of the in-between by remaining fully present to the story you're in and trusting that a plot twist in your favor is just up ahead. When a door closes but another one hasn't opened, it may feel like hell in the hallway, but hold on to hope.

Hope is often defined as a feeling or an expectation for something to happen. It is more than wishing for something; it is an active anticipation that what you are aspiring toward will come to be. Wonder gives birth to new expectations. Hope will give you the fuel to stay expectant instead of merely wishful. Wishful thinking might offer you a temporary dose of optimism, but hope combined with wonder is an unstoppable force.

When you find yourself between stories and feel like you're drowning, this magical combination will help you keep living. Literally. A gruesome experiment conducted in the 1950s sheds some light on what I mean.

Curt Richter, a professor at Johns Hopkins University, gathered a group of wild and domesticated rats, as well as some jars filled half-way with water. He was curious how long the rats would swim before they gave up. He took a dozen of the domesticated rats, put them in the jars, and then proceeded to watch them drown. *Psychology Today* describes the process of the first rat: "The first rat, Richter noted, swam around excitedly on the surface for a very short time, then dove to the bottom, where it began to swim around, nosing its way along the glass wall. It died two minutes later."[1]

Two more rats died basically the same way and in about the same amount of time. But the nine other domesticated rats? They swam for days. Naturally, they eventually gave up and drowned as well. But what about the wild rats? They were "renowned for their swimming ability. The ones Richter used had been recently trapped and were fierce and aggressive."[2] What happened next is surprising.

One by one, the wild rats were dropped into the jars of water. Every single one of them died within minutes. All thirty-four of them.

This study may seem dark, but stick with me.

When I read about this study, I wondered the same thing you're probably wondering and the same thing Richter wondered in the lab that day. Why did the tame, domesticated rats swim for days, while the wild rats died immediately?

Hope.

Richter wrote, "The situation of these rats scarcely seems one demanding fight or flight—it is rather one of hopelessness. . . . The rats are in a situation against which they have no defense. . . . They seem literally to 'give up.'"[3]

But the study didn't stop at this point. Richter tried another experiment with more wild rats. He put them also in jars of water, but just before they were expected to drown, he came to their rescue. He pulled them from the water, held them, comforted them, and then put them back into the water. Doing so communicated to the rats that their situation wasn't hopeless after all.

I love the way *Psychology Today* summarizes the final part of the research: "This small interlude made a huge difference. The rats that experienced a brief reprieve swam much longer and lasted much longer than the rats that were left alone. They also recovered almost immediately. When the rats learned that they were not doomed, that the situation wasn't lost, that there might be a helping hand at the ready—in short, when they had a reason to keep swimming—they did. They did not give up, and they did not go under."[4]

Richter echoed that by summarizing: "After elimination of hopelessness, the rats do not die."[5]

Remember in *Finding Nemo* that Dory's mantra was to "just keep swimming"? It's no coincidence that Dory's character was one filled with wonder. She was a baby fish trapped in a big fish's body. Her wonder switch was definitely on. But what about Marlin, the clown fish who wasn't funny? On top of being short on wonder, Marlin constantly ran out of hope. It was Dory's combination of wonder and hope that gave her the drive to just keep swimming.

We as human beings are unique among the living, breathing creatures in that we are in constant search of meaning. We are quite different from fish. And rats. We are also the only creatures who tell stories in an attempt to find and *create* that meaning we're searching for.

Welcome Your Weird

The search for meaning that drives us to be storytelling creatures is also what leads us to fall prey to lies and illusions. We're so desperate to find meaning that we'll make up whatever story is necessary to justify our strange behaviors. Then we convince ourselves we're living an authentic life, all while experiencing the lack of belonging we all desperately desire.

There are four things we seek: meaning, purpose, love, and belonging. The desire for these four things leads us to do some strange things, doesn't it? But here's another secret to living a life of wonder and magic: you must become comfortable with what makes you weird.

In a world of platform building and perception management and the curating of social media content, where everyone is putting on a show, far too often we cave to the pressure to lean into the status quo. Our desperation to belong drives us to want to be normal. But being "normal" would mean blending in by being like everyone else.

But you're not like everyone else. And no one else is exactly like you. You may have wanted to be yourself, but then the world told you who you were supposed to be and your true authentic self started fading away.

When your wonder switch is turned back on, you will no longer be normal. You will soon become a member of the minority of people who believe in magic. And believing in magic is weird. Isn't it?

There's no possible way to fit every lie into a single book, but if there's a lie to put on the short list inside the pages of this one, that list wouldn't be complete without a dire warning not to buy the lie that whispers, "Don't be weird." The magic you were meant to offer the world doesn't come from leaning into the status quo in an attempt to be normal. The magic you're meant to experience and use to serve others is found when you welcome your weird. In my middle school, playing sports and, more importantly, being good at them made you "cool." Magic tricks were weird. But the wonder that had been newly reawakened at the time gave me permission to embrace being a magician anyway, and that wonder became contagious to others. It wasn't at first—I wasn't the cool kid for a long time. But when you release yourself from the constraints of applause and approval, you will taste a freedom that you'll spend the rest of your life trying to preserve.

I love the story *Alice in Wonderland* by Lewis Carroll. My kids and I especially like the live-action feature film written by Linda Woolverton and directed by Tim Burton.

In the opening scene of the film, Alice is asleep in her bed. Fresh off a trip to Wonderland, she climbs out of bed and peers around the corner with a look of concern at her father, who is in the middle of a business meeting, visioneering the future. He pauses the meeting and comes back to Alice's bedside to comfort her, asking, "You had the dream again, didn't you?" Alice confirms and asks, "Do you think I've gone round the bend?" In other words, "Have I lost my mind? Am I a weirdo? Am I crazy?"

I love what happens next.

Alice's dad gets very serious, pauses, and says, "I'm afraid so. You're mad. Bonkers. Off your head." But then he leans in toward Alice with a warm, whimsical smile and says, "But I'll tell you a secret. All the best people are."

As Alice grows up, she visits Wonderland often. Later, in the same film, the Mad Hatter asks her the same question: "Have I gone mad?" Embodying the spirit of the wonder of her father, Alice puts her hands on the cheeks of the Hatter and repeats those same words: "I'm afraid so. You're entirely bonkers. But I'll tell you a secret. All the best people are."[6]

My friend, you are entirely bonkers. The reason you feel so weird when you live an authentic life is because you are. And your ability to embrace your "weird" and live as the truest version of yourself is rooted in whether your wonder switch is on or off. Awaken your wonder, and live the life you were meant to live. It's time to shift from being "liked" to learning how to simply be.

My son, compared to the "normal" kids his age, is weird. I'm doing everything in my power to help him embrace his uniqueness. Sometimes at night, after tucking him into bed, I'll look at him and say, "Jude, you're sooo weird." Instead of being offended, he'll giggle. He's fine with it because of what always comes next. I smile back at him and say, "But guess what?" And he always answers the question by saying, almost with a wink and a nod, "But all the best ones are."

Don't forget to go down the rabbit hole every now and then if you need to take a trip to your wonderland. You can close your eyes and go there anytime you want. And you'll soon discover: your "weird" is really just a well-kept secret shortcut to the wonderful life.

Unicorns Are Magic

In the world of artists, Picasso may have been one of the weirdest. Doesn't his art feel like it was created by someone who was "entirely bonkers"? I think so.

Picasso said we have to keep the inner child alive. He once asked, "All children paint like geniuses. What do we do to them that so quickly dulls this ability?"[7] I think we encourage them to be normal in an effort to spare them from bullying and shame, lest they be "weird" to those around them. Picasso more famously said, "Every child is an artist. The problem is how to remain one when we grow up."[8]

Flipping your wonder switch requires learning to view the world the way you once did, long ago, when you were a child. That childlike perspective has become one of the greatest ways I keep my wonder alive and has carried me through a wild and treacherous journey filled with ups and downs with my belief in magic still intact. And when wonder is crushed, my children repeatedly help me learn to see the magic again.

Five years after I burned my face doing the fire-breathing trick the night of that unforgettable Fourth of July, I find myself in a parking lot outside a Dave & Buster's. I'm experiencing a moment of magic so profound that it solidifies my wonder switch in the on position for a very long time.

Jude was now five years old, and he had recently discovered a new obsession: arcade games. We'd visited a cool, old vintage arcade while on a vacation, and now we were back in Nashville, and he was desperate to be back in front of some games. The only arcades in Nashville at the time were at Chuck E. Cheese and Dave & Buster's. Because I love arcade games as much as Jude does, I opted for Dave & Buster's.

Wednesdays became our guys' night for almost the entire winter. Every Wednesday night was half-price game night, and if I wasn't on the road speaking or performing, we'd take a trip to play some games.

As you may be aware, unlike arcades like Chuck E. Cheese, where you swipe your card to play a game and receive physical tickets when you win, everything at Dave & Buster's is digital. You swipe your card to pay credits to play a game, and the tickets you win are deposited digitally back onto the same card you swiped.

Week after week, Jude and I would play some games, win a bunch of tickets, and go choose a prize. And week after week, the prize Jude chose was a pack of gummy bears from the candy section. We would go in, win thousands of tickets, and he'd spend 150 of them. This was repeated for a few months, until finally, I thought, "I should probably get my son outside more often. Spring is just around the corner. Maybe we've had enough arcade games for a while."

I now explain to Jude that this will be our last time at the arcade for a while and that it would be best if we spend all his tickets. He has no concept of how many we have collected. We go to the shop to scan our card, and I can't believe my eyes. We have amassed almost 180,000 tickets. It turns out, when you come back week after week but choose only a pack of gummy bears, tickets add up.

I now explain to little five-year-old Jude that he can pick anything he wants in the entire store. "Anything?!" he asks. "Yes, anything."

Jude starts to walk around the shop. I point out his options. I show him shelves of board games, remote control trucks and cars. I walk him over to a glass cabinet filled with electronics, saying, "Look, Jude. You can even get an iPad."

He continues to walk around, eventually lifting his eyes to the top shelf that borders the entire shop. Along this shelf are giant stuffed animals, many of which are bigger than he is. You can probably imagine what we're looking at. He gradually works his way over to the corner where there's a giant, fluffy white unicorn with a hot pink mane and a golden horn. And then he speaks.

"Dad, do I have enough tickets to get that unicorn?"

Ugh. What do you say in that moment? Here's what I say: "You could. Or you could get an iPad."

Jude says, "I want to get that unicorn."

In that moment, I had a moment. As a dad, I wasn't sure what to do. Sure, we'd recently watched the Minion movies as a family and laughed at the little girl who fell in love with the same stuffed unicorn that sat on the top shelf of Dave & Buster's that day, but

I didn't expect my son to want one too. I wasn't sure what to do. I paused, then proceeded to say, "Yes, if that's what you really want. But you can have just about anything else too."

As we leave the building and walk across the parking lot toward our car to head home, Jude beams. I, on the other hand, am not. I'm not upset; I'm still perplexed. I ask, "Are you excited about your unicorn, buddy?"

With a huge smile on his face, he looks up at me and says, "Yeah, Dad. Sissy is going to love her unicorn so much."

Instantly, I take a deep breath, and it's as if it resets my whole system.

In that moment, Jude had not pulled out a deck of cards and said, "Pick a card, Dad!" I didn't watch a magic trick. There was no sleight of hand or misdirection. But I experience the golden pool of real magic. The wonder I experience performs its magical work and leaves me in tears and transformed all over again.

Real magic does that.

My son loves his sister the way that only seems right to a child. In his mind, there is no scarcity; there is only abundance, and plenty to go around. He does not have to rob others of their joy, because his is overflowing. His wonder is still wide awake, and magic is alive and well. His ability to be himself reminded me of who I am, and who I have the ability to become.

Everything You Want

You don't need to have children to have a life of magic. There are children everywhere, and even if they don't belong to you, they can teach you a lot about wonder. To a child, magic isn't just at Disney World. It isn't only in sunsets over mountaintops or even the mountaintop experiences of life. Wonder sees the extraordinary in what others assume is ordinary. It sees magic everywhere.

Let's go back to where we started—not just as children, but at the beginning of this book—by asking the same question with which we began.

What do you want?

If you had wisdom, you could attain just about anything you want, even if wisdom changes your desires along the way. And wisdom begins in wonder. Awaken your wonder, and it will be the beginning of the next chapter in the story of your life. There's nothing wonder doesn't have the power to transform. This is the end of "business as usual."

When you reach the final moments of your life, I believe the old saying is true. Your life will not be measured by the number of breaths you took but by the moments that took your breath away. That's magic. But you don't have to wait until those final moments. The magic is all around you, and it's even inside you. Wonder will permit you to see it by giving you permission to believe in what you have yet to fully see.

Let's go back and look in the mirror again. What do you see? Is there anything that leaves you in awe and wonder? Perhaps you still aren't seeing clearly, but you will.

We marvel at the stars but struggle to see magic in the mirror. And yet, as the story goes, the maker of the stars called them good, but then made you and called you "really good." How much more magic is there in you than even in the stars in the sky? It doesn't matter what worldview you hold, the answer is consistently the same: quite a bit.

I don't know what your story holds, but I hope your wonder transforms the untrue stories you've told yourself and gives birth to an epic journey, whether that's a moon shot to the stars or a journey around the world sailing the high seas. Wherever your wonder takes you, I hope you settle for nothing less than the magical life you were meant to live.

Life itself is a miracle. Sounds like a cliché you might find on a Hallmark card, doesn't it? But what if it's true? Scientists estimate that the odds of your being born are about one in four *trillion*. In a fun article for *HuffPost*, Dr. Ali Binazir challenges that stat by laying out the chances. First, what are the chances of your parents meeting? One in twenty thousand. And if that happens, what are the chances of your mom getting pregnant? One in two thousand. In that process, what are the chances of the right sperm meeting the right egg? One in four hundred *quadrillion*. And none of this takes into account the multiplication that takes place as a result of this process happening not only with your parents but also your grandparents, great-grandparents, and every generation that came before you.

When you think about it, scientists' estimate of one in four trillion sounds conservative. And as Dr. Binazir says, "A miracle is an event so unlikely as to be almost impossible. By that definition, I've just proven that you are a miracle."[9]

The tricks I perform on stages around the world are commonly referred to as magic, but are really just clever illusions. But that doesn't mean magic isn't real. This can be the beginning of a magical, creative life. Getting here required adventuring into the dark together. My hope is that you learned a lot along the way, finding your way through that darkness, and that this journey has left you better off than when you first began.

Now you know most of my secrets. I guess we're both magicians now. Use your powers wisely—they won't just change your life; they might just change the world too.

The Next Step in Your Story

Thanks for reading *The Wonder Switch*. I hope this book has encouraged you to live a life of wonder. While this page is near the end of the book, the good news is that your story does not stop here.

I'd like to invite you to join me for a mini master class where I'll dive even deeper into wonder and help you take some of the ideas we've talked about and apply them to your life in practical ways. Wonder has helped me step into a new story, and I know it can do the same for you. For this and more exclusive, free content about next steps on your path, go to www.harrisiii.com/wonderswitch.

I can't wait to hear what
happens next,

Harris III

Acknowledgments

In his book *On Writing*, Stephen King said, "Writing is not life, but I think that sometimes it can be a way back to life."[1] I didn't understand those words when I first read them, but now that I'm at this stage of the journey, I get it. The person whose life this book has changed the most is me.

I've spent a lot of time thinking about why that is. Why did the process of writing it change me? I think the answer is found less in the writing and more in the thinking—the processing that precedes the typing of the words onto the page. And once they're typed, the process that is involved in reading, editing, and rewriting those words.

When I think about that process, it's filled with a long list of people. I may have written the words on these pages, but they wouldn't have been written without those people.

Allison Fallon was one of the first to not only express belief in the ideas on these pages but also help me outline an original first draft of this book. When I mentioned that draft to Mark Classen during a catch-up at WME, he expressed the same level of belief and introduced me to my amazing literary agent, Margaret Riley King. The enthusiasm they each had for a project that had yet to be fully realized is indeed proof of the fact that believing is seeing.

Another person who believed long before there was anything to see is my editor, Stephanie Smith. She not only believed; she helped bring this book to life and has been there at every step along the way with unwavering support. This book just wouldn't be what it is without her; it may not have even ended up in your hands. Thank you to Stephanie, my copyeditor Kim Tanner, Paul Fisher, David Morris, and the rest of the publishing team at HarperCollins and Zondervan. You guys are amazing.

Special thanks to Jim Woods for helping me get unstuck so many times. Your role in this book continued to grow and grow, and now your fingerprints are all over it, cover to cover. Kristen Samuel, Danielle Bennette Simmons, and Bart Green all left their magical fingerprints all over it as well.

Special thanks to Marc Pimsler for helping me write responsibly. The amount of time you committed to assisting with this book as I neared the finish line still leaves me in awe. Thank you for your wisdom, insight, and generosity.

Thanks to David Paull, Gina Derickson, and the team at Engagious for helping with some insightful research that led to a lot of key understanding. David, I can't wait to read your book on behavioral storytelling. Those of us in pursuit of a life of wonder will learn much from you.

Thank you to all the amazing friends who discussed this book and its ideas over long calls, texts, meals, and backstage conversations. It's quite a list of amazing folks, including Kevin Carroll, John Bucher, Chad Cannon, Chris Petescia, Shannon Scott, Jason Jaggard, Ken Black, Michael Margolis, Linda Woolverton, Seth Bible, Chad Jarnigan, Vera Leung, Brad Montague, Ben Stewart, and many more. Thanks to each of you for your friendship.

Thank you to the STORY family for your unwavering

inspiration. Leading this community is something I don't take lightly. You're changing the future.

Thanks to my assistant, Ashlye Underwood. I wouldn't have been able to finish this book without your assistance or your ability to help protect my schedule and carve out the time I needed to write.

And thanks most of all to my wife, Kate, and Jude, Everly, and Mylo. There are no words that suffice—only tears of joy and gratitude for the role each of you has played. Thank you for your patience and sacrifice as I've worked so many days and long nights on this project. You keep my wonder alive and help me keep believing in magic.

Notes

Chapter 1: Wonder Switch On

1. Sandra M. Meier et al., "Increased Mortality among People with Anxiety Disorders: Total Population Study," *British Journal of Psychiatry* 209, no. 3 (September 2016): 216–21, https://doi.org/10.1192/bjp.bp.115.171975.
2. Tracy Shawn, "How Awe Can Diminish Anxiety," PsychCentral, July 8, 2018, https://psychcentral.com/blog/how-awe-can-diminish-anxiety/.
3. Erin Parker, "Educators: Make Room for Brad Montague," *HuffPost*, April 5, 2017, https://www.huffpost.com/entry/educators-make-room-for-brad-montague_b_58e53f17e4b0ee31ab953427.
4. Attributed to Joseph Campbell, https://quoteinvestigator.com/2013/05/23/campbell-treasure/.

Chapter 2: Wonder Switch Off

1. "Understanding and Preventing Child Abuse and Neglect," American Psychological Association, 2009, http://www.apa.org/pubs/info/brochures/sex-abuse.aspx.
2. Robert R. McCammon, *Boy's Life* (New York: Simon and Schuster, 1991), 3–4.

Chapter 3: The Old Story

1. Ron Marshall, "How Many Ads Do You See in One Day?" Red Crow Marketing Inc., September 10, 2015, https://www.redcrowmarketing.com/2015/09/10/many-ads-see-one-day/trackback/.
2. "Data Never Sleeps 5.0," Domo, accessed May 15, 2020, https://www.domo.com/learn/data-never-sleeps-5?aid=ogsm072517_1&sf100871281=1.

3. Jonathan Gottschall, *The Storytelling Animal: How Stories Make Us Human* (New York: Houghton Mifflin Harcourt, 2012), back cover.
4. Gottschall, *Storytelling Animal*, 56.
5. Keith Oatley, "The Mind S Flight Simulator," *Psychologist* 21 (December 2008): 1030–33, https://thepsychologist.bps.org.uk /volume-21/edition-12/mind-s-flight-simulator.
6. Gottschall, *Storytelling Animal*, 58–59.
7. "What Is the Kuleshov Effect?" Lights Film School, https://www .lightsfilmschool.com/blog/what-is-the-kuleshov-effect-agj.
8. Quote commonly attributed to Seth Godin.
9. Seth Godin, "Putting a Value on a Story," *Seth's Blog*, May 10, 2018, https://seths.blog/2018/05/putting-a-value-on-a-story/.
10. Tomas Higbey, "What Are the Best Stories about People Randomly (or Non-randomly) Meeting Steve Jobs?" Quora, July 1, 2013, https://www.quora.com/What-are-the-best-stories-about-people -randomly-or-non-randomly-meeting-Steve-Jobs/answer/Tomas -Higbey.
11. Roald Dahl, *The Minpins* (New York: Viking Penguin, 1991), 48.

Chapter 4: Reawakening Wonder

1. Jill Suttie, "How Awe Brings People Together," *Greater Good*, July 3, 2017, https://greatergood.berkeley.edu/article/item/how_awe _brings_people_together.
2. J. K. Kiecolt-Glaser et al., "Emotions, Morbidity, and Mortality: New Perspectives from Psychoneuroimmunology," *Annual Review of Psychology* 53 (2002): 83–107, https://doi.org/10.1146/annurev .psych.53.100901.135217.
3. Kiecolt-Glaser et al., "Emotions, Morbidity, and Mortality."
4. Jake Abrahamson, "The Science of Awe," University of California Berkley Psychology, 2014, https://psychology.berkeley.edu/news /science-awe.
5. J. E. Stellar, "Positive Affect and Markers of Inflammation: Discrete Positive Emotions Predict Lower Levels of Inflammatory

Cytokines," *Emotion* 15, no. 2 (April 2015): 129–33, https://doi
.org/10.1037/em00000033.

6. "The Power of the Placebo Effect," Harvard Health Publishing,
last modified August 9, 2019, https://www.health.harvard.edu
/mental-health/the-power-of-the-placebo-effect.

7. "The Power of the Placebo Effect."

8. Mark B. Abelson, MD, and Kate Fink, "Controlling for the Placebo
Effect," *Review of Ophthalmology*, April 17, 2003, https://www
.reviewofophthalmology.com/article/controlling-for-the
-placebo-effect.

9. A. Khan, N. Redding, and W. A. Brown, "The Persistence of the
Placebo Response in Antidepressant Clinical Trials," *Journal of
Psychiatric Research* 42, no. 10 (August 2008): 791–96, https://doi
.org/10.1016/j.jpsychires.2007.10.004.

10. Marlena A. Piercy et al., "Placebo Response in Anxiety Disorders,"
Annals of Pharmacotherapy 30, no. 9 (September 1996): 1013–19,
https://doi.org/10.1177/106002809603000917.

11. R. Eccles, "The Powerful Placebo in Cough Studies?," *Pulmonary
Pharmacology and Therapeutics* 15, no. 3 (2002): 303–8, https://doi
.org/10.1006/pupt.2002.0364.

12. Tim Newman, "Is the Placebo Effect Real?," Medical News Today,
September 7, 2017, https://www.medicalnewstoday.com
/articles/306437.php.

13. Marisa Peer, "Reprogram Your Mind through Affirmations:
Marisa Peer," Mindvalley Talks, March 1, 2019, YouTube video,
1:00:55, https://www.youtube.com/watch?v=L57HYnWVNfk.

14. It is debated whether Henry Ford ever said these exact words, but
by research of Quote Investigator, it isn't a stretch. The words echo
other similar quotes and writings from those who came before
him. https://quoteinvestigator.com/2015/02/03/you-can/.

15. I have seen these words credited to multiple sources, both online
and in print. I first heard of them from a leadership podcast by
author, speaker, and pastor Andy Stanley.

16. Dr. David Benner, *Soulful Spirituality: Becoming Fully Alive and Deeply Human* (Grand Rapids: Brazos, 2011), 161.

Chapter 5: A New Story

1. Mark Twain, *A Connecticut Yankee in King Arthur's Court* (CreateSpace Independent Publishing, 2018), 422.
2. "Fears: Summary of Story 2019: Attendee Survey," Engagious, 2019.
3. Randy L. Buckner et al., "The Brain's Default Network: Anatomy, Function, and Relevance to Disease," *New York Academy of Sciences* 1124 (2008): 1–38, http://www.nslc.wustl.edu/courses/Bio3411 /woolsey/Readings/Lecture11/Buckner%20et%20al%202008.pdf.
4. George Sylvester Viereck, "What Life Means to Einstein," *Saturday Evening Post*, October 26, 1929, http://www.saturdayeveningpost .com/wp-content/uploads/satevepost/what_life_means_to _einstein.pdf.
5. Viereck, "What Life Means to Einstein."
6. Sir Ken Robinson, "Sir Ken Robinson - The Power of Imagination," Inspiration Journey, April 24, 2020, YouTube video, 5:14, https:// www.youtube.com/watch?v=ol-70F5nzc0.
7. Robinson, "The Power of Imagination."
8. I first heard this phrase from my friend Jason Jaggard, who gave a great talk about the dark side of the imagination at STORY conference. Check it out at www.storygatherings.com.
9. Brené Brown, *Daring Greatly: How the Courage to Be Vulnerable Transforms the Way We Live, Love, Parent, and Lead* (New York: Penguin Random House, 2012), 255.
10. Ichiro Kishimi and Fumitake Koga, *The Courage to Be Disliked: How to Free Yourself, Change Your Life and Achieve Real Happiness* (New York: Atria, 2013). Gives a great introduction to Adlerian psychology in an easily digestible format.
11. Joseph Campbell, *The Power of Myth* (New York: Anchor, 1988), 161.
12. Yes, where eagles cry on a mountain high ;)
13. Steven Pressfield, *The War of Art* (New York: Grand Central, 2002), 25.

14. Check out Allison's amazing talk given at STORY 2018 on the power of developing a practice of writing regularly, regardless of whether you have ambitions to be a "writer." Go to storygatherings.com.

15. Creativets Songwriting, https://creativets.org/songwriting/.

16. Scott Barry Kaufman, "Turning Adversity into Creative Growth," *Scientific American*, May 6, 2013, https://blogs.scientificamerican .com/beautiful-minds/turning-adversity-into-creative-growth/.

17. Matthew W. Reynolds, Laura Nabors, and Anne Quinlan, "The Effectiveness of Art Therapy: Does It Work?," *Art Therapy* 17, no. 3 (2000): 207–13, https://doi.org/10.1080/07421656.2000.10129706.

18. "How to Manage Truama," National Council for Behavioral Health, 2012, https://www.thenationalcouncil.org/wp-content/uploads /2012/11/Trauma-Infographic-Print.pdf?daf=375ateTbd56.

19. Henry David Thoreau commonly attributed quote, source unable to be located.

20. "The Power of Imagination," Glebe Montessori School, June 9, 2014, https://www.glebemontessori.com/the-power-of -imagination-3/.

Chapter 6: The Wonder Mindset

1. Carol S. Dweck, PhD, *Mindset: The New Psychology of Success* (New York: Penguin Random House, 2006), 17.

2. Dweck, *Mindset*, 6.

3. Dweck, *Mindset*, 6.

4. Dweck, *Mindset*, 10.

5. This quote is commonly attributed to both Eleanor Roosevelt and Theodore Roosevelt, but no source was able to be found.

6. Remy Melina, "Are We Really All Made of Stars?," Live Science, October 13, 2010, https://www.livescience.com/32828-humans -really-made-stars.html.

7. "The Neuron," BrainFacts.org, April 1, 2012, https://www.brainfacts .org/brain-anatomy-and-function/anatomy/2012/the-neuron.

8. "Functional Plasticity," APA Dictionary of Psychology, American

Psychological Association, https://dictionary.apa.org
/functional-plasticity.

9. Marc Bangert and Eckart O. Altenmüller, "Mapping Perception to Action in Piano Practice: A Longitudinal DC-EEG Study," *BMC Neuroscience* 4, no. 26 (2003), https://doi.org/10.1186/1471-2202-4-26.

10. Daniel L. Schacter et al., "The Future of Memory: Remembering, Imagining, and the Brain," *Neuron* 76, no. 4 (November 2012), https://doi.org/10.1016/j.neuron.2012.11.001.

11. Tom Bilyeu, "Why Mindset Is Everything: Tom Bilyeu | Rich Roll Podcast," Rich Roll, February 26, 2019, YouTube video, 2:22:48, https://www.youtube.com/watch?v=prlqWU54NME.

12. Jessica Stillman, "Gratitude Physically Changes Your Brain, New Study Says," *Inc.*, January 15, 2016, https://www.inc.com/jessica-stillman/the-amazing-way-gratitude-rewires-your-brain-for-happiness.html.

13. Dan Baker, PhD, *What Happy People Know* (Kutztown, PA: Rodale, 2003), 86.

14. Marianne Williamson, *A Return to Love: Reflections on the Principles of "A Course in Miracles"* (New York: HarperCollins, 1992), 190–91.

Chapter 7: Creating Wonderland

1. Mark D. Griffiths, PhD, "Testing the Atmosphere," *Psychology Today*, February 1, 2013, https://www.psychologytoday.com/us/blog/in-excess/201302/testing-the-atmosphere.

2. Bob Goff, "Cynicism is fear posing as confidence; joy is hope let off the leash," @LoveDoes, Facebook, January 6, 2014, https://www.facebook.com/bobgoffis/posts/577416119000332.

3. Tsung-Ming Tsao et al., "Health Effects of a Forest Environment on Natural Killer Cells in Humans: An Observational Pilot Study," *Oncotarget* 9, no. 23 (March 2018), https://doi.org/10.18632/oncotarget.24741.

4. Qing Li, "Effect of Forest Bathing Trips on Human Immune Function," *Environmental Health and Preventive Medicine* 15, no. 1 (March 2009): 9–17. https://doi.org/10.1007/s12199-008-0068-3.

Chapter 8: Wonder in Action

1. John F. Kennedy, "Address at Rice University on the Nation's Space Effort," (speech, Rice University, Houston, TX, September 12, 1962), https://er.jsc.nasa.gov/seh/ricetalk.htm.

2. Kennedy, "Address at Rice University."

3. "July 20, 1969: One Giant Leap For Mankind," NASA, July 20, 2019, https://www.nasa.gov/mission_pages/apollo/apollo11.html. These famous words are actually "That's one small step for man. One giant leap for mankind." But both Neil Armstrong and the official NASA transcript report the words to be "one small step for a man."

4. Lillian Cunningham, *Moonrise* podcast description, iTunes, https://podcasts.apple.com/us/podcast/moonrise/id1469151663.

5. "Benefits from Apollo: Giant Leaps in Technology," NASA, July 2004, https://www.nasa.gov/sites/default/files/80660main_ApolloFS.pdf.

6. Albert Einstein commonly attributed quote, source unable to be located.

7. Leonardo da Vinci's diaries cited in Michael J. Gelb, *How to Think Like Leonardo da Vinci: Steven Steps to Genius Every Day* (New York: Delacorte, 1998), 50.

8. "Joint Meeting of the Two Houses of Congress to Receive the Apollo 11 Astronauts, Congressional Record," September 16, 1969, https://www.hq.nasa.gov/alsj/a11/A11CongressJOD.html.

9. Louis Armstrong commonly attributed quote, source unable to be located.

10. Charles J. Limb and Allen R. Braun, "Neural Substrates of Spontaneous Musical Performance: An fMRI Study of Jazz Improvisation," *PLOS One* 3, no. 2 (February 2008), https://doi.org/10.1371/journal.pone.0001679.

11. Eleanor Roosevelt in Elaine Partnow, *The Quotable Woman, 1800–on* (New York: Macmillan, 1978), 193.

12. Ken Robinson commonly attributed quote, source unable to be located.

Chapter 9: Right Your Story

1. Joseph T. Hallinan, "The Remarkable Power of Hope," *Psychology Today*, May 7, 2014, https://www.psychologytoday.com/us/blog/kidding-ourselves/201405/the-remarkable-power-hope.

2. Hallinan, "The Remarkable Power of Hope."

3. Curt P. Richter, "On the Phenomenon of Sudden Death in Animals and Man," *Psychosomatic Medicine* 19, no. 3 (May 1957): 191–98.

4. Hallinan, "The Remarkable Power of Hope."

5. Richter, "On the Phenomenon of Sudden Death," 196.

6. *Alice in Wonderland*, written by Linda Woolverton, directed by Tim Burton (Walt Disney, 2010).

7. Quote commonly attributed to Pablo Picasso.

8. Attributed to Pablo Picasso, https://quoteinvestigator.com/2015/03/07/child-art/#note-10748-2.

9. Ali Binazir, "Are You a Miracle? On the Probability of Your Being Born," *HuffPost*, June 16, 2011, https://www.huffpost.com/entry/probability-being-born_b_877853.

Acknowledgments

1. Stephen King, *On Writing: A Memoir of the Craft* (New York: Simon and Schuster, 2000), 249.